'No matter how many house chores you complete, there are always more to be done.'

African Proverb

Jen Chillingsworth

CLEAN GREEN

Tips and recipes
for a naturally clean,
more sustainable
home

Illustrations by Amelia Flower

Hardie Grant

QUADRILLE

Publishing Director Sarah Lavelle
Commissioning Editor Harriet Butt
Series Designer Gemma Hayden
Junior Designer Alicia House
Illustrator Amelia Flower
Head of Production Stephen Lang
Production Controller Nikolaus Ginelli

Published in 2020 by Quadrille, an imprint
of Hardie Grant Publishing

Quadrille
52–54 Southwark Street
London SE1 1UN
quadrille.com

Cataloguing in Publication Data: a catalogue
record for this book is available from the
British Library.

Text © Jen Chillingsworth 2020
Illustrations © Amelia Flower 2020
Design and layout © Quadrille 2020

ISBN 978 1 78713 502 4

Printed in China

FSC
www.fsc.org
MIX
Paper from
responsible sources
FSC® C020056

Contents

Introduction

Walk along any cleaning aisle in a supermarket and you will find a vast range of products on offer. From ironing water, laundry whiteners and floral-scented disinfectants to antibacterial surface wipes, there is a cleaning product for every conceivable problem area in the home. I used to love exploring the cleaning aisle, often enticed by the intriguing perfume combinations that promised the aroma of springtime, ocean breeze or fresh linen. My kitchen cupboards groaned with bottles, sprays and wipes, yet I would always buy more, eager to try something new. I never took any time to consider the amount of plastic I was buying, or that the cloths I used released tiny microfibres into the water supply or that the sponges I bought ended up in landfill. When I decluttered my cleaning cupboard, I was stunned to find I had almost thirty of those pesky laundry detergent washing balls lurking in the back. I had never paid the slightest attention to any of it.

Everything changed for me when I was admitted to hospital after accidentally inhaling a bleach-based cleaning product. Even though I had followed the instructions carefully, worn rubber gloves and ventilated the room well, the strength of the product had overwhelmed my system. Thankfully I was okay, but this incident made me question what was in these products, and what I was regularly exposing my family to as well. Out went the toxic products made from unpronounceable chemical combinations and synthetic fragrances and I made the switch to greener commercial alternatives.

Our homes should be the haven we retreat to at the end of a busy day, provide us with comfort during

the dark, cold days of winter and be a place where we can nurture our loved ones. We want to keep our homes clean, yet many of us are regularly exposing ourselves and our families to high levels of indoor air pollution simply by using a cleaning product or spraying an air freshener. Before I changed to greener products, my home was full of toxins that I didn't think twice about. In the kitchen, I would wash my dishes with a regular dishwashing liquid, I'd fill the washing machine with liquid detergent and fabric conditioner, disinfect the kitchen floor and wipe down all the surfaces with an antibacterial wipe which I'd then throw in the rubbish bin. Every time I vacuumed the living-room carpet, I'd sprinkle a little carpet-cleaning powder over it first. The plug-in air freshener would repeatedly release a jasmine and honeysuckle scent and I'd burn scented candles made from paraffin wax. The bathroom would be cleaned with a power cleaning spray, the toilet would be bleached, and I'd fight an endless battle trying to get the

mildew out of the shower curtain. All these products were releasing harmful toxins into my home and we were breathing them in every single day.

Look at the back of any commercial cleaning product and some of the first words you will see are 'caution' or 'danger', often followed by an exclamation mark. These are not only warnings regarding your safety and wellbeing; they are also highlighting the harm they can do to the environment. Many of the ingredients in these products are derived from non-renewable sources like petroleum, and they are not biodegradable. When we do laundry, we are releasing synthetic chemicals and tiny microfibres into the water supply, where they can be ingested by marine life and potentially enter the human food chain. Burning candles made from paraffin fills our indoor air with synthetic fragrances and fumes that are comparable to those from a diesel engine. Air fresheners, glass cleaners, furniture polish and even wet wipes release harmful VOCs (volatile organic compounds), such as formaldehyde, into the air in the home, which can lead to serious health conditions in the short and long term. Waste products like sponges, scouring pads and blue cleaning cloths are all made from plastic and take hundreds of years to break down. Toilet and cleaning wet wipes get flushed down the toilet where they can end up causing severe damage to sewage systems.

As I researched deeper into the green alternatives, I discovered that there were even better, healthier choices to commercial green cleaning products and there were some great ways to cut down on waste, too. Both play a vital role in cleaning the home naturally and in helping to reduce our environmental impact. I clean my home very differently now. I make most of my own natural cleaning products, I buy reusable tools that are biodegradable or compostable, and I look to reduce my waste as much as possible too. Let's be honest – cleaning is not fun, but it doesn't have to complicated. In this book you'll find simple, practical ideas to help you 'green clean' your home. From laundry detergent and furniture polish to making your own natural air freshener, they are easy to make and they work. They are not expensive, and many will save you money in the long term. Every recipe I make uses only a few ingredients and you will find many of them in your local supermarket or easily available online. I've detailed each individual ingredient in the first section of this book so you can be clear on what role it plays in the recipes that follow.

It's important to add that we are all at different stages of our lives or have different needs and not everyone can make all their own cleaning supplies. Accessibility, work or family commitments often take up a lot of our resources, energy and time. If this is you, then why not begin with one or two of the ideas in this book that you can easily incorporate into your daily routine? I believe small steps lead to big changes and every single change can only be a good thing for our wellbeing and the wider environment.

Getting Organized

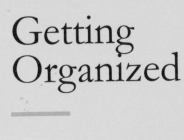

*'A good system shortens
the road to the goal.'*

Ralph Waldo Emerson

Getting organized

It isn't always easy to keep on top of cleaning your home. Life is busy and sometimes we let things slide. I used to leave all the cleaning in my home until the weekend, cramming it all in between running to the grocery store and taking my son on playdates or visiting family. Everything was done in a haphazard manner with no planning and there were always things I missed. Consequently, I often resorted to using stronger products to shift the grime.

Over the years I've learned to simplify things and make better decisions about what I bring into my home, but there was a lot of trial and error before I found the way that works well for us. The important thing to remember is not to feel discouraged if you can't do it all perfectly. There is no right or wrong way; there is only the way that works best for you and your household.

I believe everyone who lives in the home should be responsible for keeping it clean and tidy. If you are in a relationship, then aim to divide up the tasks fairly. In my house, although I do most of the cleaning, my husband cooks, irons and washes up. If you live with roommates, again divide the tasks and agree on a rota. Teaching kids how to clean and look after their own home is a great life skill to pass on. Get them involved by encouraging them to tidy away toys and look after their bedrooms. Invest in a small dustpan and brush set for little hands to learn to sweep up after themselves. Ask older children to make their beds, clear the table and help with the washing up. By creating a plan that works for you, as well as making more considered choices about what you buy, green cleaning can be simple. Over the next few pages you'll find some easy ways to help you get started.

Conscious cleaning

I'M NOT GOING TO PRETEND THAT I ENJOY CLEANING BECAUSE I REALLY DON'T. YET ONCE I SWITCHED TO GREEN CLEANING, I FOUND IT MORE BEARABLE.

No longer was I breathing in toxic fumes, buying hundreds of products or discarding things to landfill. Instead, I was making considered choices about what I was bringing into my home. I spent time researching what I was using, from how products were made and the resources required for their manufacture and supply to how the wider environment could be affected by the choices I made. I've come to think of this as conscious cleaning.

Along with the five r's which you can find on page 18, the six points listed opposite sum up the key principles we should all consider when we clean consciously.

NO MORE TOXINS

Air pollution from cleaning products in our homes cause harm to our wellbeing and to the wider environment. Many commercial cleaners have been found to contain carcinogens, hormone disrupters and mood-altering chemicals. When you switch to nontoxic cleaning recipes, you will be safe in the knowledge that what you are using will not harm you, your family, your pets or the environment.

USING RESOURCES

Switching to these green cleaning recipes means you are opting to use ingredients that are renewable or are naturally occurring resources not in danger of running out.

CONSERVATION

Become more mindful of water consumption and the energy that you use to clean your home. Only run the dishwasher when it's completely full, turn down the temperature on the washing machine or run it on a cold cycle, and use grey water (the dirty water left behind in the sink from dishwashing) on the garden.

LESS IS MORE

By cutting down on the amounts of products you buy, you will also vastly reduce your consumption of plastic bottles and tools, which ultimately end up in landfill and can take hundreds of years to break down. Choose concentrated products and bulk buy whenever possible, which could end up helping you to save money too.

CLEANER WATERWAYS

Commercial cleaners are full of toxic chemicals that can leach into the water supply and harm aquatic lifeforms. None of the recipes in this book will cause any harm to waterways or the lifeforms that depend upon them.

ANIMAL TESTING

Many commercial cleaning products are tested on animals either by the manufacturer or by third parties. By switching to green cleaning recipes, you are ensuring that no animal has been harmed in any way.

How to begin

THERE ARE THOUSANDS, IF NOT MILLIONS, OF GREEN CLEANING RECIPES TO BE FOUND ONLINE AND OFTEN THE INFORMATION THEY PROVIDE IS CONFLICTING.

Many don't explain their purpose or recommend using ingredients that are difficult to comprehend. Some mix together ingredients that end up working against one another, effectively cancelling one another out. It's important to understand why and when to use certain ingredients in green cleaning recipes, so before you begin, I strongly recommend that you read the health and safety notes on page 24 and Chapter 3 on ingredients (pages 38–69).

Here are some other points to consider before you start green cleaning:

USE UP WHAT YOU HAVE
Whether it's a bottle of dishwashing liquid, laundry detergent or even a plastic scouring pad, the greenest way to dispose of it is to use it up. However, if you are keen to get started and have any unopened cleaning products, donate them to a local food bank.

START SIMPLE
My advice is to take it slowly and change one thing at a time. It's useful to see how a recipe performs for you before changing anything else. I began by making a basic multipurpose kitchen spray (see page 74). This recipe takes only seconds to make, costs very little and is extremely effective. Using the spray for a few weeks and seeing how successful it was encouraged me to move on to the next recipe I wanted to try.

BE REALISTIC

If you are short on time or find that it's not practical to create a cleaning recipe for every area of your home, then that's okay! Instead, make whatever recipes you can and use them alongside commercial green cleaning products. Every small change makes a difference, so try not to worry about what you can't do and instead, embrace what you can do.

Think about habits that you could change to become more sustainable. Could you reduce your energy consumption or switch to a renewable energy supplier? How about reducing the amount of water you use? Try running a shorter programme on the washing machine or filling the kitchen sink only half full before you wash the dishes. Changing how you shop is also a good way to be more sustainable. Look for stores that offer refillable green cleaning products, where you can take your own containers. Make this part of your shopping routine instead of relying on grocery stores.

The five r's

It's important to look at all the ways you can make a difference when you are green cleaning, from responsible consumption and conservation of energy to the amount of waste you produce.

A really simple way to approach this is to think about the five r's: refuse, reduce, reuse, recycle and rot. By applying these guiding principles, you can make better sustainable choices for your home and lifestyle.

Here are a few ways you can use the five r's to help become a more eco household:

REFUSE
Do not buy products that will ultimately end up in landfill. From plastic sponges and blue cleaning cloths to disposable wipes, these are all products that we need to stop buying and discarding.

REDUCE
Learn to stop making impulse purchases and only buy what you need. Don't purchase lots of things that will never get used and look at how you can create less waste overall. If a small appliance breaks down, rather than replacing it, take it to a repair café run by volunteers who will help you to fix it for a small contribution. Look online for a repair café near you.

REUSE
Turn jam jars, nut butter jars or instant coffee jars into storage jars for dried goods such as bicarbonate of soda (baking soda) and citric acid (remember to label them). Use small glass drinks bottles for any cleaning recipe that calls for a spray gun (see page 36). Old cotton t-shirts can be cut up into cleaning rags.

ROT

You can compost many of your green cleaning tools, such as replaceable dishwashing brush heads made from tampico fibres, bamboo toothbrushes (with the nylon bristles removed), reusable organic cotton sponges or natural rubber gloves. You can also add any dust or hair from sweeping or vacuuming, and old newspapers used for cleaning glass can also be torn up and added to the compost bin. Several recipes in this book use sprigs of herbs and citrus peels as ingredients, all of which can be added to the compost heap after straining.

RECYCLE

Whatever you can't refuse, reduce or reuse. Check online to see what items your local authority will accept for recycling.

Weekly cleaning rhythm

A HOME IS A RETREAT FROM THE OUTSIDE WORLD. IT IS THE PLACE WHERE WE SEEK COMFORT, CREATE MEMORIES AND NURTURE OUR FAMILY.

A home needs to be cared for too, yet we often lack the time or energy to do so.

Creating a cleaning rhythm can help you to maintain the balance in your home. Working to that rhythm allows you to keep on top of things and free up your time elsewhere.

If you have lots of rooms to tackle or if you live in a studio apartment, your rhythm will probably look very different to mine. You can reassess your rhythm if it's not working well for you, or your circumstances change. That's perfectly okay – the goal isn't perfection, but finding a balance that works for you, the number of people in your home and your lifestyle.

HERE'S HOW TO START:

» Make a list of all the tasks you need to complete in your home.

» Decide how frequently these tasks need to be completed.

» Make it easier for yourself – is there a time of day or specific day that will work better for you? It may be 15 minutes in the evening or before you go to work.

» Once you've worked out what needs to be done, split the tasks up into the days of the week that work best for you. I stick up a printout of our rhythm so that everyone in our home can see it.

This is my weekly rhythm

Things I do daily

» *Kitchen*: wipe down the sink, countertops and tabletop. Wash the dishes. Sweep the floor after main meals.

» *Bathroom*: wipe down the sink with an organic cotton cloth.

» *Bedrooms:* make the beds (allow your beds to air for an hour with the covers turned back before you make them as this allows any moisture to dry out and deters dust mites).

» *Laundry*: try to do one load of laundry per day. I like to load the machine the night before, switch it on first thing in the morning and hang it outside to air dry before I begin my working day.

Things I do weekly

» *Kitchen:* wipe down appliances. Clean cooker and hob (stovetop). Sweep and mop the floor.

» *Living room:* dust and wipe down appliances. Dust and polish furniture. Water houseplants. Vacuum.

» *Bathroom:* clean and disinfect the toilet. Scrub the bathtub and sink. Clean the shower, mirrors and accessories. Wash the floor. Change and launder the towels and bathmat.

» *Bedrooms:* change and launder the bedding. Dust and tidy. Vacuum.

Seasonal cleaning

Following a cleaning rhythm can help you stay on top of daily and weekly tasks (see page 21), but sometimes a deeper clean is necessary to prevent things getting out of control.

Traditionally known as spring cleaning, I prefer to think of it more as seasonal cleaning – taking the time to refresh the home whilst embracing the new season. In spring I change heavy winter-weight duvets over to lighter ones and deep-clean carpets, whereas when the days begin to shorten and temperatures drop it's time to layer up with woollen blankets and prepare the fire. However, no matter what the season, there are specific jobs that are worth doing every three months, so try to include these in your seasonal cleaning plan.

TASKS FOR ALL ROOMS

Start at ceiling level and work your way down to the floor, rather than working upwards, because as you clean dust will drop to the lower levels. Work from one side of a surface to the other, lifting objects as you go.

Dust and wipe down light fittings, cabinets, window frames, curtain rods, and door frames, removing cobwebs as you go. Move on to mid-level areas like doors, blinds (shades), chairs, bookshelves, lamps, media units, radiators and appliances. At floor level, dust skirting boards (baseboards), vents and radiator pipes.

Wash any curtains and air dry. Look for a green dry-cleaning service if you have curtains that cannot be laundered at home. If you have houseplants, wipe down all pots, remove any dead leaves and give plants a lukewarm shower (only for plants in pots with drainage holes) to remove dust from their leaves. This helps houseplants counteract poor humidity and photosynthesize more efficiently.

Tasks for specific areas:

LIVING ROOM
Shake out rugs and vacuum under the sofa. Declutter magazines, books, DVDs, ornaments, etc.

KITCHEN AND LAUNDRY
Clean the tops of cupboards, refrigerators and open shelving. Declutter the kitchen cupboards, drawers, freezer and refrigerator. Clean and disinfect the coffee machine and other appliances.

BEDROOM
Declutter your closet, chest of drawers and bedside table. Clean the mattress (above opposite). Flip and rotate your mattress. Change and wash your duvet. Clean under the bed. If you have children declutter and clean their toy boxes and launder any soft toys.

HOW TO CLEAN A MATTRESS
Scatter a little bicarbonate of soda (baking soda) over the mattress and gently rub it in with your hands. Leave for 30 minutes before vacuuming up all the powder. If you wish, add lavender essential oil to the bicarbonate of soda before you sprinkle it on to the mattress – this helps promote better sleep and repels dust mites.

BATHROOM
Clean and disinfect shower curtain rods and shower head. Remove dust from inside the bathroom extractor fan and declutter any storage units. Clean children's bath toys using the castile spray on page 74.

Health & safety information

ALTHOUGH ALL THE INGREDIENTS IN THESE CLEANING RECIPES ARE NONTOXIC, THEY ARE STILL CHEMICALS AND SHOULD BE TREATED WITH PROPER CARE AND ATTENTION.

Make sure you read each recipe thoroughly and follow all instructions for use. Many people can have allergies or reactions to nontoxic products, so keep a note of the new products you are using. If any ingredient or recipe gets on your skin or in your eyes, rinse immediately with clean water.

TEST
Always carry out a spot test on a surface that you want to clean. Choose an inconspicuous area (perhaps in a corner, on the back or underside) and using a tiny amount of the product, check that it is safe to continue. If any problems arise, rinse immediately with clean water and do not continue to use on that surface. Ventilation – open doors and windows before cleaning to extract any fumes.

SPONGES
Keep any sponges used for dishwashing separate from sponges used to clean other areas of your home. Disinfect regularly.

RUBBER GLOVES
Always wear rubber gloves before mixing any ingredients together as well as during the actual cleaning process to avoid skin irritation. I use natural rubber gloves that can be composted once they come to the end of their lifespan – but be aware that they are made with latex, which can cause allergies for some people.

STORAGE

Keep all ingredients in sealed containers and label them clearly. Don't put any cleaning products where young children or pets can access them.

ESSENTIAL OILS

Some essential oils should not be used if you are pregnant or have young children or pets. Please refer to page 63 for further details.

EQUIPMENT

See page 34 for information on using separate equipment for food preparation and making cleaning products.

Mixing ingredients and commercial cleaning products together is not a good idea as they can often work against one another and in some cases, be extremely dangerous:

VINEGAR AND CASTILE SOAP

If combined they will directly cancel one another out, leaving behind a white, curdled oily mixture.

BICARBONATE OF SODA (BAKING SODA) AND VINEGAR

Although not harmful, bicarbonate of soda is a base and vinegar is an acid so when they are mixed, they essentially neutralize one another to form water and salt. The recipes in this book often use both ingredients, but never at the same time.

VINEGAR AND BLEACH

Combining these two can make toxic chlorine gas, which can cause chemical burns and respiratory problems. If you are still using bleach in your household, treat it with extreme caution.

Green Cleaning Tools

*'You don't get anything clean without
getting something else dirty.'*

Cecil Baxter

Green cleaning tools

We need tools to help us complete the task of cleaning our homes, yet we don't always consider the impact these have on the environment because we focus purely on the products we are using. Plastic sponges, scouring pads, all-purpose blue cloths and plastic dishwashing brushes end up in landfill where they will take hundreds of years to degrade. Microfibre cloths release tiny microplastic particles into our water supply every time they are laundered. Antibacterial wipes get used once before being flushed away into the sewage system, where they can cause serious blockages or find their way into the ocean.

Rather than continue buying these tools and increasing your plastic consumption, make the switch to green cleaning tools. There is a huge selection of products to choose from and most are derived from renewable resources and are biodegradable or compostable. Alternatively, you could simply repurpose what you already own – old cotton t-shirts or shirts can be cut up and made into cleaning cloths, glass bottles can be reinvented as cleaning spray containers, coffee jars or jam jars can be used to store your natural cleaning recipes, and an old bamboo toothbrush is great for cleaning tough spots. If you are at all crafty, then try making your own dishcloth using leftover yarn – there are lots of online tutorials to show you how.

Over the next few pages, you'll find out what I recommend and use regularly to clean my home with. There is also an essential equipment list for the items you will need to make the recipes in this book.

Green cleaning utensils

These are the tools that I use regularly for cleaning all areas of my home. Not only are they better for the planet but most importantly, they do the job I ask of them. I buy my tools from online retailers, independent hardware stores and, more recently, at my local zero-waste store.

SCOURING PADS

Look for pads made from loofah or walnut shells as they are naturally abrasive and won't scratch surfaces. Plant-based sponges take less energy to produce and completely break down when thrown away. Wash by hand between use and dry thoroughly.

COPPER CLEANING CLOTH

Copper is a soft and non-abrasive metal and these cloths clean pans, glass, steel, sinks and stoves very gently. Pop them in an old sock or a cotton mesh bag and launder them in the washing machine and they can then be reused many times. They are also 100% recyclable.

REUSABLE SPONGE

Choose cotton and bamboo sponges with an outer hessian (burlap) layer as this provides an abrasive texture to help clean pots and pans. I use these to clean countertops, sinks and the bathtub. They are machine washable and if you look after them properly, they will last for months. Once they come to the end of their lifespan, cut them up and add them to the compost bin.

ORGANIC COTTON CLOTHS

Most commercially available cleaning cloths are made from cotton, which is a major source of environmental pollution. Switching to organic cotton significantly reduces the amount of water used in the production process and no harmful pesticides or herbicides are required in farming. They are biodegradable and compostable. I use organic cotton cloths for most of my spray recipes. (And, as mentioned on page 28, old t-shirts can be used as cleaning cloths too.)

WOODEN DISHWASHING BRUSH

Look for brushes that have replaceable heads with bristles made from tampico fibre. Be aware that many wooden dish brushes come with bristles made from horse hair, which are not vegan friendly. Tampico fibre is derived from the agave plant and is both biodegradable and compostable.

GROUT AND TILE BRUSH

Made from bamboo and recycled plastic, this has two sets of bristles – stiff ones to get into the grout and softer bristles to clean the tiles.

COTTON MOP

I use a wooden handled mop with a removable, washable cotton head. After I've cleaned the floor, I pop the cotton head in the washing machine and then air dry. Make sure that the mop head is completely dry before putting away because a wet mop can harbour bacteria.

GALVANIZED MOP BUCKET

Look for one with a fixed internal conical wringer that you can use to squeeze out your mop between strokes. These buckets are extremely durable and can last a lifetime. *continued »*

LAUNDRY PEGS

Most plastic and wooden clothes pegs (clothes pins) sadly don't last very long. The next time you need to replace them, switch to stainless steel clothes pegs as they are strong, durable and won't rust. Alternatively, choose traditional wooden dolly pegs that have FSC (Forest Stewardship Council) certification, which means that the trees used have been felled and managed responsibly.

Buy only what you need

There are many companies who try to capitalize on the 'sustainability trend', but you don't need an array of sleek amber glass bottles and fancy label makers to store your cleaning products in, nor do you need to have a beautifully styled kitchen to display them in. If you want to be truly sustainable, use up what you already have and only buy when you really need to replace something.

DO A QUICK STOCKTAKE OF YOUR CURRENT CLEANING EQUIPMENT.

If you already have lots of microfibre cloths, keep using them rather than buying new organic cotton ones. The same applies to packs of scouring pads, dishwashing brushes and plastic sponges. Once you have used everything up, think about making the switch to the green cleaning equipment I've listed on pages 30–32.

ASK YOURSELF WHAT DO YOU REALLY NEED TO CLEAN YOUR HOME?

If you live alone, you won't need an enormous array of equipment or supplies as your home won't be subject to quite as much daily wear and tear as a family home with young children. Try to work out how many of each item you will realistically need before you stock up. We are a family of three, yet before I set off on my *Clean Green* adventure I had a kitchen cupboard with over thirty cloths, and I probably only used around a third of them.

WHEN YOU DO HAVE TO BUY SOMETHING, LOOK FOR SECOND-HAND OPTIONS.

Dustpans and brushes, feather dusters, rattan rug beaters, dish towels and glass jars for storing your recipes can regularly be found at car boot sales (yard sales) and charity shops (thrift stores) for next to nothing. Pick up glass bottles, jars and china teacups from vintage fairs and use them as storage vessels or candle holders. Borrow or rent what you don't own or regularly use. For example, ask a friend or neighbour if you can borrow their steam-cleaning mop (you could return the favour by gifting them a bottle of one of your home-made cleaning recipes). Steam cleaners and carpet cleaning machines can also all be hired for a day.

Rather than buy something yourself, why not ask for it as a gift for Christmas, birthday, house-warming or a wedding? A simple wooden clothes dryer, a bar of Savon de Marseille soap or an enamel dustpan are all great presents to give or receive.

Equipment for recipes

It's a good idea to gather together a few essential pieces of equipment before you start making any of the recipes in this book.

Many of these items are things that you may already have in your kitchen, but be sure to keep them separate from anything you use for food preparation purposes.

RUBBER GLOVES

It's extremely important always to wear gloves when you are mixing cleaning materials. I buy ethically sourced natural rubber gloves as once they come to the end of their lifespan, I can cut them into strips and add them to the compost bin.

MIXING BOWL

Invest in a good-quality, heat-resistant glass bowl. Certain recipes like the liquid laundry detergent (see page 100) call for the ingredients to be melted and it's important that you have a bowl that can withstand higher temperatures without cracking.

GLASS STORAGE JARS WITH LIDS

I like to use large Kilner jars (750-ml and 1-litre sizes) or Mason jars (16-oz and 32-oz sizes) with rubber seals for any recipes that I make in bulk, such as laundry detergent or dishwashing liquid (see pages 100–103 and 74). These jars can be reused and replacement rubber seals can easily be purchased if necessary. For any product that I make in small amounts, I repurpose old jam jars.

GLASS BOTTLES WITH TRIGGER SPRAY/PUMP

Either make your own from a glass bottle and add a trigger spray (see page 36) or invest in some amber glass bottles that you can find online or in zero-waste stores.

LABELS OR A GLASS PEN

You need to be able to identify your cleaning recipes easily so use a label maker or print out labels for this purpose. I prefer to use a glass pen to write on my jars and bottles as it's quicker and less wasteful.

SCALES

Either manual or digital scales will do. I use my glass mixing bowl instead of the scale pan, resetting the scale back to zero each time. If you prefer, measuring cups can be used for smaller quantities, but don't use the same set for measuring food.

SAUCEPAN

Choose a pan that allows your glass bowl (see opposite) to fit snugly over the rim without letting the water touch the bottom of the bowl.

HAND GRATER

Invest in a small hand grater that is only used for cleaning recipes.

SPOONS

I have a collection of enamel tablespoons that I use for mixing cleaning recipes, but several wooden spoons will do just as well. Write on the spoons with a marker pen to identify which recipe you use them for.

FUNNEL

Filling jars and bottles with your cleaning recipes can get messy and using a funnel makes everything far easier. Before you buy, measure the tops of your jars and bottles so that you can be sure that the funnel will fit properly. Stainless steel is the best option as it's durable and won't rust. Look online at preserving or home-brewing websites as they usually carry a wide selection of sizes.

Make your own spray bottle

Rather than buying new glass bottles to use for cleaning recipes, it's a simple and more sustainable option to repurpose a bottle you may already have in your home.

However, avoid using plastic spray bottles that once contained commercial cleaning products as no matter how well you wash them, there is always the risk that some residue of the original product may remain, and this can contaminate any natural cleaning product you add to the bottle.

Using a glass bottle that once contained water or a soft drink is ideal for converting into a cleaning spray.

To make the cleaning spray you will need to buy a new trigger spray, which you can find in refill stores and from online retailers. I find the trigger sprays to be small, so single-use products such as tonic water or ginger beer bottles work best because they have a slim bottle neck.

**MAKES 1 BOTTLE
YOU WILL NEED:**

» 1 glass cordial/tonic
   water bottle

» 1 trigger spray

1 Wash your bottle in
hot, soapy water. Remove
any product labels. Dry
thoroughly.

2 Cut the stem of the trigger
spray so that it reaches
just above the bottom of
the bottle. You don't want
it to touch the bottom as
that would prevent liquid
travelling up the stem
properly. However, try not
to cut the stem too short as
you will end up with leftover
liquid at the bottom.

3 Attach the trigger to the
stem and twist to fit. Fit to
the bottle neck.

4 Add a sticker, label or use
a glass pen to identify the
cleaning product your bottle
will contain.

You could also convert larger
glass bottles and add a pump
top that you can use to
dispense dishwashing liquid,
handwash or liquid laundry
detergent. Distilled white
vinegar or olive oil bottles are
good options to use for this
purpose. Wash in warm soapy
water and dry thoroughly
before filling with your
cleaning product and adding
the pump dispenser.

Green Cleaning Ingredients

'Dirt is only matter in the wrong place.'
Henry John Temple

Ingredients

It's important to understand what each ingredient is made of and the role it plays in green cleaning before you start making any recipes. Most recipes use three basic ingredients – vinegar, liquid soap and bicarbonate of soda (baking soda) – and this may seem a little repetitive when you are reading the instructions. However, the key is learning which ingredients work well together and knowing the order in which to use them to get the best results.

There are a few things to think about when buying ingredients. If you have the storage space, then consider buying in bulk. Castile soap and distilled white vinegar can be easily bought online in 5-litre (5-quart) bottles.

Soda crystals (washing soda), citric acid and bicarbonate of soda are readily available in large bags up to 25kg (55 lb), helping to reduce the need for plastic packaging. If you are fortunate enough to live near a zero-waste store, you can take along your own containers or bottles and fill them with loose ingredients like bicarbonate of soda and liquid castile soap. Health-food shops are great places to source unwrapped bars of soap and other green cleaning essentials.

Over the next few pages you'll find details on each ingredient, from how it's made and the most sustainable way to buy it to its main purpose in green cleaning.

Greenwashing

IT'S NOT ALWAYS
PRACTICAL OR
POSSIBLE TO MAKE
ALL THE CLEANING
RECIPES FEATURED
IN THIS BOOK.

Choosing commercial green
cleaning products to complement
your homemade ones is a good
compromise, but how can you
be sure which commercial products
have the best credentials? Many
companies market their products
as kind to the environment, yet
often this is far from the truth.
Known as 'greenwashing', this
sales technique tricks the
consumer into believing that the
company is doing more to protect
the environment than it really is.

The simplest way to determine
how green a product is, is to
research it. In the UK, the
Ethical Consumer website
(www.ethicalconsumer.org) offers
detailed analysis of household
products, including supermarket
own brands. In the US, the
EWG (Environmental Working
Group, www.ewg.org) has a
scoring system that highlights
how toxic a cleaning product
is. Both are independently run,
non-profit organizations helping
consumers to make better choices.

Social media can play a vital role
in highlighting when a brand is
greenwashing, too. Investigate
the hashtag #greenwashing on any
social media platform and you'll
discover a wealth of information
regarding products and brands.

INGREDIENTS TO WATCH OUT FOR:

Many cleaning recipes online use borax as an ingredient, but I've chosen not to include it in this book. It is an ingredient that divides the green-living community due to its eco credentials, and it has been banned in the EU as it was considered hazardous to health (it has been replaced with borax substitute). If you want to find out more about borax or borax substitute, then I'd advise spending some time doing your own research to determine whether you want to incorporate it into your own green cleaning routine.

It is also important to consider the use of palm oil in green cleaning. This industry has contributed significantly to climate change, from deforestation and air pollution to loss of habitat for endangered species. Palm oil is mainly found in bar soap, laundry detergents and liquid castile soap, so be sure to choose products that are free from the oil or made with certified sustainable palm oil.

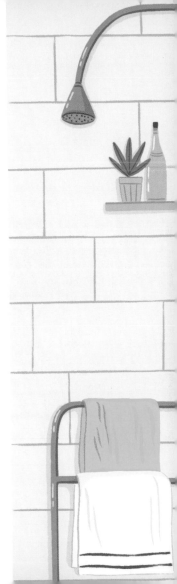

Vinegar

Alongside bicarbonate of soda (baking soda) and liquid castile soap, distilled white vinegar is one of the most important ingredients in green cleaning. It's completely nontoxic and biodegradable with a multitude of uses. It's also extremely economical and readily available at grocery stores, making it the simplest ingredient with which to start your green cleaning journey.

When I started looking into making my own cleaning recipes, I was confused by the term distilled white vinegar. It's generally not written on the labels here in the UK, but after a lot of searching, I discovered that it's also known as distilled malt vinegar or white vinegar and its name varies from country to country. Do make sure to buy the clear distilled malt vinegar rather than the brown version, or you could end up with some nasty staining.

Distilled white vinegar is made from grain-based (usually barley or corn) ethanol, which is then converted to acetic acid and diluted with water. Most of the distilled white vinegars you find in the supermarket have an acidity level of 5% and you can also find online stores that sell a more powerful cleaning vinegar with a higher acidity level of 6–8%. Either vinegar will work for green cleaning purposes, but I tend to use the 5% acidity as it's easy to pick up a bottle at your local store.

White vinegar is a natural degreaser, deodorizer and disinfectant. It has antiseptic and antifungal properties and is great at cleaning glass, dissolving soap scum and removing difficult stains. The only downside to vinegar is the smell when you are using it. Thankfully this does disappear, and you can add herbs or citrus or essential oils to combat this.

If you are looking to cut down on the amount of packaging you use and you have the storage space, you can find white distilled vinegar online in 5-litre (5-quart) containers. Alternatively, choose glass bottles over plastic ones when you purchase vinegar from the grocery store because glass is easier to recycle.

Note: Don't use vinegar on marble or granite work surfaces or stone floors as they are porous, and the acid can damage the natural stone. And if you are starting out on your green cleaning journey and still using bleach to clean your toilet, do not use vinegar at the same time as when combined they make chlorine, a toxic gas. Find out more on this in the health and safety information on page 24.

Bicarbonate of soda

Bicarbonate of soda (baking soda) is produced by mining two naturally occurring minerals, nahcolite and trona. These are refined into soda ash (calcium carbonate) and then turned into sodium bicarbonate (bicarbonate of soda). When sodium bicarbonate is dissolved in water it forms an alkaline solution, which makes it ideal for cutting through grease, dirt and oil. It is also a fungicide because it neutralizes acids that encourage bacteria.

Known as bicarbonate of soda in the UK, in the US it's packaged as baking soda. It is the same product that you would find in the baking aisle at your local supermarket, but purchasing it in these small quantities can be costly and it is often packaged in plastic too. I usually buy mine in a 500-g (1 lb 2-oz) recyclable cardboard box from a local hardware store or at a refill store where I can fill my own container. Alternatively, you can find it in bulk-sized bags online which can help to save on excess packaging.

Bicarbonate of soda (baking soda) is an effective but gentle abrasive to use on ceramics, in the sink or bathtub and to clean kitchen work surfaces. It also fights limescale, softens water and helps to combat mould problems.

For laundry, bicarbonate of soda is good for whitening and brightening or dealing with tough stains, such as sweat and grease spots. It is a natural deodorizer and is often used to freshen bins or refrigerators. Sprinkling a little bicarbonate of soda under the litter in a cat litter box can help to keep strong odours under control. If smelly shoes are a problem, add a little bicarbonate of soda to the insoles and leave overnight before emptying out the powder in the morning.

For dirty marks on painted walls, mix equal parts of warm water and bicarbonate of soda to make a paste. Using a clean cloth, dab a little of the paste onto the mark and rub gently to remove the stain.

Bicarbonate of soda is also ideal for cleaning children's toys. Mix a little bicarbonate of soda in a bowl with warm water until the powder has dissolved. Moisten a reusable sponge in the solution, wipe each toy and leave to air dry.

Note: Bicarbonate of soda that comes in a box or loose in a refill store is usually not packed in a safe-for-food environment as the companies who produce it are often manufacturing other cleaning products too. For anything edible that needs bicarbonate of soda, choose the packet from the bakery aisle at the grocery store. If you are vegan, be aware that some companies who produce bicarbonate of soda do test on animals or use third-party companies to do so on their behalf. Check with individual brands on their policies before purchasing.

Castile soap

Of all the green cleaning ingredients I use, liquid castile soap is by far my favourite. It is highly concentrated and, because a little goes a long way, it's extremely cost effective too. Pure castile soap contains no synthetic preservatives, detergents or foaming agents. It is completely nontoxic, biodegradable and safe to use around pets and children.

Originating from Spain, castile soap was traditionally made with pure olive oil, but it is now more commonly produced by mixing vegetable oils such as hemp, avocado, jojoba and coconut. It has a multitude of purposes, from cleaning floors and bathtubs to laundry detergent, because it can lift dirt and cut through grease. The soap is very gentle and can be used for bathing and shampooing hair, and even washing the dog! For green cleaning, I always tend to choose liquid castile soap as it is the easiest and more convenient option to use in recipes. You can use the bar soap too, simply by grating the soap and then diluting it in water to obtain the liquid equivalent, but this means more preparation time is required and getting the concentration right can be difficult. The solid bar does come in handy as a stain-removal tool as you can simply rub the stain with the bar to help remove it prior to washing.

Castile soap has a high mineral content and, if used in hard water, may leave a powdery residue or soap scum. This does not mean that the soap has damaged the surface and the residue can be easily removed with an extra rinse using a clean cloth.

To clean woodwork like skirting boards (base boards) or cabinet doors, add 50ml (3 tablespoons) of castile soap to a bucket of hot water. Dampen a clean cloth in the solution and wipe down any woodwork. However, avoid using on waxed or oiled surfaces.

You can find liquid castile soap in most health-food stores, but sadly most is packaged in plastic bottles. I buy mine from a local refill store and take along my own bottle to fill up, which is by far the greenest option. However, if you don't have access to refillable soap, choose the largest size of bottle you can afford or will fit in your cleaning cupboard. This helps to reduce packaging concerns and saves money too. Search online for bulk buy options.

Be sure to choose castile soap that is free from palm oil (see page 43) or uses certified sustainable palm oil as an ingredient and avoid any brands that use artificial dyes, foaming agents or synthetic fragrances. Castile soap is vegan – it is not tested on animals and it contains no animal fats, unlike many commercial soap bars.

Savon de Marseille

Produced in Marseille in the south of France for over 500 years, Savon de Marseille is a hard soap made from vegetable and olive oils. It is still produced in a unique way, with the oils, alkaline ash from sea plants and water from the Mediterranean Sea heated in antique cauldrons before being poured into open pits and left to harden. It is then cut into cubes and stamped with its weight in grams, the percentage of olive oil it contains and the maker's name to confirm its authenticity.

Traditionally, Savon de Marseille blocks are either coloured green or white. The green is made from using olive oil, whereas the white is made using palm oil. Ideally, for cleaning and washing, it is better to use a green bar that is stamped with 72% as this guarantees the percentage of olive oil in the soap. French households have been using the soap for hundreds of years to clean their homes and wash their clothing.

Savon de Marseille is a very gentle cleaner that can be used in many ways at home. From laundry powder and dishwashing liquid to cleaning floors, it is naturally antibacterial and hypoallergenic. It is completely nontoxic and safe to use around both pets and children. Savon de Marseille is unscented, but you can add some essential oils to the recipes if you prefer a scented product.

As there is nowhere local for me to purchase the soap, I buy it online as a large 600-g (21-oz) block packaged in paper. I grate the bar to make liquid laundry detergent and to use as a dishwasher powder, and use it directly on fabrics to get out difficult stains. A block lasts a long time as you need very little for effective cleaning power. Savon de Marseille is suitable for vegans, but be careful not to purchase fake bars as these often contain animal fats. Always check that you are buying an authentic product which has the traditional stamp embedded in the soap.

You can also buy Savon de Marseille flakes in paper bags. These are unscented, and free from any artificial colours or additives. They are extremely gentle and ideal for washing delicate fabrics like woollens and silks, as well as baby clothes.

If you have indoor plants and struggle to get rid of aphids, Savon de Marseille makes a great insecticide. Add a handful of grated Savon de Marseille to a glass bowl filled with 1 litre (1 quart) of warm water. Stir continuously to dissolve and allow the solution to cool. Using a funnel, pour the mixture into a spray bottle. Apply weekly if you have an infestation and make sure to spray both the upper and lower leaves of the plant. However, avoid using this spray on sensitive plants such as ferns and succulents.

Citric acid

Citric acid is a weak organic acid that is naturally present in citrus fruits. However, the acid that is used in green cleaning has been synthetically produced by the mould-based fermentation of sugars. This results in a crystallized white powder that is nontoxic and biodegradable. Citric acid is an effective disinfectant and good at killing mould or mildew. It is antibacterial, antifungal and completely odourless.

If you have hard water stains in the toilet, citric acid is a game changer. Start by adding one large tablespoon of citric acid to the toilet bowl. Do not flush and leave overnight. In the morning, use a wooden toilet brush to give the bowl a quick clean before flushing. The water will wash away any remnants of the citric acid in the bowl along with any mineral deposits, leaving your toilet sparkling.

Citric acid is also used to descale taps (faucets) and shower screens. Dissolve 2 tablespoons of citric acid in 1 litre (1 quart) of hot water and add the contents to a spray bottle (see page 36). Spray onto the surface and leave for ten minutes, then rinse clean with warm water. This simple mixture can also be used to clean kitchen work surfaces and tables.

Citric acid is sold in hardware stores or online. I only use citric acid for cleaning the toilet, so I buy a small box which lasts me a long time. If you choose to use it regularly for dealing with difficult hard water stains or cleaning shower screens, then I'd recommend buying it in bulk to help cut down on packaging and transportation. You can also find refill stores which sell it loose for you to take home in your own containers. Some citric acid is derived from genetically modified corn sucrose, so look for brands that are certified non-GMO.

Always wear rubber gloves when mixing or using citric acid as it is a skin irritant. Do not mix citric acid with bleach or soda crystals (washing soda). Always ventilate the room when you use citric acid and avoid inhaling it as it can induce coughing or shortness of breath. Keep away from children and pets.

Many online green cleaning recipes recommend using citric acid as the base for making toilet bombs. These are formed by mixing citric acid and bicarbonate of soda (baking soda) with a few drops of essential oils, then moulded into shapes. Although they are pretty, they have no real purpose other than to fizz when they react with water. Citric acid is more effective when used on its own. See the toilet freshening powder on page 125 for a quick recipe to use for toilet freshening.

Note: Citric acid must not be used on marble worksurfaces or stone flooring as the acid can seriously damage the porous surface. Avoid using citric acid on brass taps (faucets) or fixtures as it could tarnish the metal and do not use on enamel and aluminium.

Soda crystals

Soda crystals (washing soda) are used in many green cleaning recipes as they have excellent degreasing power and help to soften hard water. They are biodegradable, nontoxic and contain no enzymes, phosphates or bleaching agents. Washing soda is a fine white powder and when added to water produces soda crystals.

Known as the chemical compound sodium carbonate, soda crystals/washing soda are closely related to sodium bicarbonate (bicarbonate of soda/baking soda). Both are derived from the naturally occurring mineral trona (see page 46) but they are used in different ways for green cleaning. Sodium carbonate is very alkaline, with a pH of 11, and this high alkalinity helps to raise the pH level of water and boost a detergent's effectiveness.

Soda crystals are very effective at removing difficult stains like red wine or coffee from clothing if pre-soaked in a hot water and soda crystal solution. They are fantastic for keeping your washing machine clean as they help to remove limescale and detergent build-up. I mostly use soda crystals in my natural laundry powder recipes (see page 102) as they are an excellent water softener and brightener. The crystals bind to hard water minerals, allowing the detergent to clean fibres and lift stains.

Soda crystals are widely available in the laundry section of most supermarkets or local hardware stores. Here in the UK, they are mostly to be found packaged in 1-kg (2 lb 4-oz) plastic bags or online in bulk 10-kg (22-lb) options. They are packaged in plastic because soda crystals are a water-based product and in high temperatures the crystals can clump together and melt. However, in other countries, washing soda in powder form can be found in cardboard boxes or in paper sacks. UK readers can find washing soda in powder form online.

Use soda crystals regularly to prevent sinks becoming blocked. Pour a large cup of soda crystals down the plughole, then flush with hot water. Soda crystals are abrasive, and they can scratch delicate surfaces, so use them with care. Don't use on aluminium or lacquered surfaces.

You can use soda crystals (washing soda) to give appliances a good clean. Add 100g (½ cup) to 500ml (2 cups) warm water and let dissolve. Dip a clean cloth in the solution and wipe down the refrigerator, cooker hood, washing machine, dishwasher, etc. Avoid using on any aluminium or lacquered surfaces. This solution also works well for cleaning venetian blinds, patio furniture and plastic shower curtains.

Note: Be sure to wear rubber gloves when mixing or during use as the soda crystals can cause skin irritation. Unlike bicarbonate of soda, soda crystals must not be consumed as they are caustic. Keep out of reach from children and pets.

Soap nuts

Not actually a nut but a fruit, soap nuts closely resemble shrunken, wrinkled walnut shells. They can perform a multitude of tasks around the house, are nontoxic and can be reused several times. Once they come to the end of their lifespan, they can be popped in the compost bin as they are 100% biodegradable. Soap nuts are gentle, hypoallergenic and extremely economical. They have antibacterial, antifungal and antimicrobial properties too.

Soap nuts grow on the *Sapindus Mukorossi* tree, a species native to Nepal and India. The trees take nine years to yield their first crop, but once they start producing the berries can be harvested for more than six months of the year and, incredibly, each tree can fruit for over 90 years. Soap nuts contain a natural soap called saponin, which tastes unpleasant to insects, so no harmful pesticides or herbicides are needed for their production. To harvest the crop, farmers gather berries that have fallen from the trees. The seeds are then removed and replanted. The soap nut shells are cleaned and dried in the sun, with no chemical processing necessary.

Soap nuts are most commonly used as a natural laundry detergent. The saponin in the soap nuts is released in water, helping to lift dirt and grime from fabric. To use soap nuts, simply pop a small handful in a muslin bag and add to the drum of the washing machine. Soap nuts are odourless, but you can use a few drops of essential oils on the bag, which helps to scent the laundry. One bag of nuts can be repeatedly used until they stop soaping, usually after four to six washes. To check if they are spent, simply squeeze the shell and if any soapy liquid is released, they can be reused again.

Washing at low temperatures prevents the nuts from soaping properly, whereas hot water is more effective and this, of course, means more energy is required. If you have babies or young children who get dirty easily, be aware that soap nuts are not good for stain removal and a long pre-soaking treatment will be necessary for tough stains (wash at least 40°C degrees).

Soap nuts can also be used to wash dishes – see page 82 for instructions on making a soap nut tea which can be used for handwashing dishes and in the dishwasher.

This soap nut tea can be used to clean windows and work surfaces. Simply add the solution to a spray bottle, squirt and rinse off with a clean cloth. Windows will benefit from a rub down with an old newspaper after cleaning. Pop the soap nut tea in the refrigerator to prevent it from turning bad. It should remain fresh for around three weeks. Alternatively, divide the mixture and freeze in individual portions. Defrost before using.

You can find soap nuts in health-food stores and online. Look for 100% certified organic and fair-trade brands.

Lemons

Lemons are simply fantastic for green cleaning as they are naturally antibacterial. The oils contained in the peel have disinfecting properties and release an uplifting scent. Lemons come in particularly useful when dealing with mineral build-up or cutting through grease, and they are highly effective at tackling limescale. Lemon peel, slices and juice can all be used for green cleaning, making them a great zero-waste option. Buy lemons loose from the grocery store or the market. If you have a lot of them and they aren't going to get used immediately, simply freeze them. Zest the peel and freeze in ziplock bags or containers. Squeeze the juice and pour it into ice-cube trays to give you handy individual portions for cooking or cleaning. Defrost before using. In the laundry, lemons make powerful stain removers and are great at getting rid of yellow sweat stains. They also work well for brightening white fabrics – soak white clothing overnight in water and add the juice of half a lemon, in the morning rinse and launder as usual.

I like to add some lemon peel or slices to a jar with distilled white vinegar (see page 116) to make a simple and economical disinfectant. Leave the peel or slices to infuse in the vinegar for 3–4 weeks, then remove and add them to the compost bin.

Use a lemon to kill bacteria that may linger on wooden chopping boards. Firstly, wash the chopping board and rinse. Next, scrub the surface with the cut side of a lemon and set aside for 10 minutes. Finally, rinse with hot water and leave to air dry. Wooden utensils can also be cleaned this way.

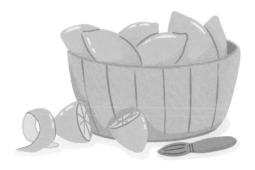

Got a stained and smelly plastic toilet seat? Rather than resorting to bleach or buying a new toilet seat, scrub the offending stains with half a lemon, cut side down. Rinse well. You may have to repeat this several times if the stains have been there a while.

If you have a small amount of stained grouting, try cleaning it with lemon juice. Soak a reusable sponge in the juice of a lemon and apply to the affected area. Rinse thoroughly with warm water. It may take a couple of applications or a harder scrub using an old bamboo toothbrush or grout cleaning brush (see page 31). For a more intensive cleaning recipe to deal with dirty grout and tiles, refer to page 122.

Try rubbing a cut lemon over a plastic food container to help shift tough stains.

It's not essential to buy organic or unwaxed lemons for green cleaning. However, buying organic means that less or no pesticides will have been used in the farming of the fruit. Wash both waxed and unwaxed lemons before you use them for any of these recipes.

Salt

You probably already have a box of salt in your larder to use in cooking, but perhaps you didn't realize that salt makes an excellent green cleaner too. It is highly effective at stain removal because of its ability to soak up moisture and, due to its abrasive nature, it works well as a gentle scouring agent. Salt is nontoxic and biodegradable.

There are a lot of cleaning recipes online that use Epsom salts instead of table or sea salt as an ingredient. Epsom salt is a mineral compound known as magnesium sulphate and it is most commonly used in beauty and healthcare. If you have hard water in your area, avoid using Epsom salts as they can add more minerals and make the water even harder. Magnesium in water can also interfere with the cleaning action of soap or detergent and reduce their effectiveness. Choose table or sea salt for green cleaning. I always have a box of sea salt to hand on my kitchen counter for use when cooking. I buy a small box from the grocery store which, despite having a plastic bag inside, is a better choice than the plastic tub that most table salt is packaged in. I've yet to find a refill store locally that sells it loose, but there are online plastic-free stores that package it in paper. Look for a refill store near you or join a zero-waste group on social media who can advise you on what's available in your area.

From an environmental point of view, sea salt is the better option as it is still traditionally produced by evaporation from the sun and wind. There are many traditional producers of sea salt around the world so search online for the one closest to you. Table salt, however, is typically extracted through mining and then evaporated in a vacuum. This uses more energy than traditional sea salt practices and, because most table salt is imported from the Far East, transportation must be considered too. By supporting a local sea-salt business, both energy and transportation will be significantly reduced.

Got a red wine stain? Don't try to rub it out. Instead, soak up as much of it as you can with a reusable cloth before covering the whole stain with salt. Leave overnight, and then launder as normal.

Salt mixed with lemon juice is great for getting rid of stains on fabric caused by rust. Sprinkle a teaspoon of sea salt over the stain. Squeeze a lemon and pour the juice over the salt. Leave to dry in the sunshine and then rinse with cold water. Wash as normal.

Essential oils

What does clean smell like to you? Perhaps it's the intoxicating bouquet of a sweet summer rose or the woody redolence of a forest. These popular scents are often included in commercial cleaning products, but they are not natural. Instead, they are artificially created by scientists in a laboratory and these toxic chemicals cause harm to the environment and contribute to air pollution in your home.

Cleaning products don't need to have a fragrance in order to do their job. It's the other ingredients used that perform that vital role. However, if you like your home and laundry to have a scent, you can make your own using essential oils.

Extracted from aromatic plants by steam distillation or by cold pressed expression, essential oils are highly concentrated and extremely potent. They must be diluted in water or a carrier oil before use and only a few drops are needed at a time. Many oils have the added benefit of being naturally antibacterial, antiviral and antiseptic.

When you are choosing essential oils, wherever possible buy pure organic oils to guarantee the plant was not sprayed with herbicides or pesticides as these can pass into the oils during steam distillation.

Look for companies that use native plants and share their origins on their labels, e.g. tea tree from Australia or lavender from the UK. Cheaper oils are often diluted and may not have been produced sustainably, whereas pure essential oils are more expensive. Buy bigger bottles as this uses less packaging and saves money, too.

Rainfall, climate and the right soil conditions allow native species of plants to grow well without intervention, whereas non-native plants may need extra water, artificial light and heat as well as chemical fertilizers added to the soil. Monocropping and deforestation are other environmental issues to consider when choosing essential oils. Research brands to find out what their policies are on farming and human rights issues before you buy. It's worth noting that several plants used for essential oils are threatened with extinction, including frankincense, sandalwood and rosewood, so avoid using these if possible.

Over the page you'll find my favourite essential oils and the blends that I use for green cleaning. However, if your budget is tight, I suggest only using one or two. Tea tree and one of the citrus oils will provide you with both antibacterial and antiseptic benefits and release a wonderful scent throughout your home.

Notes: If you are pregnant, please discuss with a midwife or healthcare advisor before using as some oils are not safe to use during pregnancy. Pet owners should note that many essential oils, including tea tree, are not safe to use around your furry friends, so speak to your vet before you use any essential oils in the home. Always store essential oils out of sunlight and away from pets and small children.

Essential oil blends

HERE ARE THE BLENDS OF ESSENTIAL OILS I USE IN MY GREEN CLEANING RECIPES. MANY HAVE NATURAL DISINFECTING AND ANTIBACTERIAL PROPERTIES, WHILE OTHERS MAKE MY HOME SMELL INCREDIBLE.

» *Basil*: (herbal) spicy and peppery scent, uplifting

» *Geranium rose*: (floral) stimulating and uplifting

» *Grapefruit:* (citrus) light and zesty scent, fresh and reviving

» *Lavender*: (floral) relaxing

» *Lemon:* (citrus) fresh, clean scent, antimicrobial, disinfecting

» *Orange:* (citrus) fresh, fruity scent

» *Peppermint*: (herbal) antibacterial, good disinfecting properties

» *Pine*: (herbal) pine-needle scent, antimicrobial

» *Roman chamomile*: (herbal) fruity and herbal scent, used to soothe and calm

» *Rosemary*: (herbal) medicinal, disinfecting

» *Tea tree*: (herbal) warm and spicy scent, antiseptic, antimicrobial and antifungal

» *Eucalyptus:* (herbal) natural disinfectant and antiseptic. Repels dust mites.

» *Clove:* (spicy) naturally cleansing and a good disinfectant.

» *Ginger:* (spicy) antiseptic and antibacterial properties. Good at deterring insects.

As essential oils can be expensive, I suggest starting slowly and only buying one oil at a time. Lemon is ideal as it has a lovely fresh smell and it's a natural disinfectant. I'd then add to that an essential oil that has antibacterial or antiseptic properties, such as tea tree or peppermint. You can use lemon and tea tree or peppermint for almost all the green cleaning recipes in this book. Simply switch the listed ingredients in each recipe for the oils you have. If you look again at this list of oils, you will see each essential oil has a scent group which I've highlighted in italics. This information is useful if you want to create your own blends and the general rule is that if the oils belong to the same scent group, they will complement one another.

If you want to get more creative, then the following scent groups also work well together:

» *Citrus & Floral*
» *Citrus & Herbal*
» *Floral & Herbal*
» *Spicy & Citrus*

The previous blends are for beginners and so are a good place to start, whereas the recipes below are more advanced.

These are my favourite blends and I use them in several recipes in this book:

» *Grapefruit, basil & peppermint*
» *Chamomile & orange*
» *Geranium rose & lavender*
» *Lemon, lavender & peppermint*
» *Orange & rosemary*
» *Peppermint & lemon*
» *Pine & lemon*
» *Rosemary, sage & lavender*
» *Tea tree & lemon*

There are no strict rules regarding how many drops of each oil you should use in a blend. Some essential oils are much stronger than others and more expensive, too. For every recipe in this book I've listed the number of drops of essential oils that I use, but this can easily be adjusted to find the combination that works best for you.

Fresh herb & citrus peel powder

Some recipes in this book use freshly dried herbs and citrus peel made into powders. The herbs and citrus peel add scent naturally, so if you can't or don't want to use essential oils, these make a great alternative.

Lavender, mint, rosemary and thyme are good options for the herb powder as they are all highly aromatic even when dried and they don't rot easily. Once you have dried the herbs, you can make separate powders or mix them together to create your own scent combinations.

I tend to choose grapefruit and lemons to make the citrus peel powder because these are readily available at my local greengrocer. Any citrus fruit will work as a powder, so feel free to experiment and come up with your own recipe ideas.

How to dry citrus peel

1 Wash and dry the citrus fruit. The skin is only used as a natural fragrance so washing it in cold water is fine.

2 Using a vegetable peeler, remove the coloured part of the skin, leaving the white pith behind.

3 Place the peeled strips on a plate, peel side down. Leave the peel to dry for 3–4 days at room temperature. After that time they will be shrivelled and ready to use.

How to dry fresh herbs

1 Cut sprigs of herbs and remove any leaves that are in poor condition.

2 Wash the herbs and gently pat dry in a cloth or tea towel (dish towel).

3 Remove the lower leaves at the bottom of the sprigs, then bundle the stems together and tie with twine or an elastic band.

4 Cover the bundles with a muslin cloth or a paper bag, poking several holes in the muslin cloth or bag to allow air circulation.

5 Hang the bundles somewhere warm and dry, making sure the leaves point downwards. Air drying herbs takes approximately 10 days.

How to make a herb and/or citrus peel powder

1 Strip the leaves from the dried herb bundles and add them to a food processor or coffee grinder.
and/or

2 Take the dried strips of citrus peel and add them to a food processor or coffee grinder.

3 Keep pulsing until the herbs/peels form a fine powder.

4 Store in a tightly sealed, labelled container.

Other ingredients

There are a few other ingredients that I use in these green cleaning recipes. Although they are not used regularly, it's good to learn a little more about them and the purpose they fulfil.

VEGETABLE GLYCERINE

A by-product of soap manufacturing, glycerine is derived from coconut, soy, rapeseed, corn or palm. It is a thick, clear syrup that is used as a natural preservative, but it is also good at removing dirt and stains. Look for organic vegetable glycerine and choose brands that don't use palm oil in their ingredients list.

FRACTIONATED COCONUT OIL

Made by removing the fatty acids from virgin coconut oil. Fractionated coconut oil is light, odourless and liquid at room temperature. As demand for coconut oil has intensified, environmental problems have dramatically increased too. Coastal mangroves have been cleared for coconut monocropping, pesticides are being used and vital ecosystems have been destroyed. However, organic coconut farming uses no pesticides or herbicides and biodiversity remains healthy. Choose recyclable glass bottles of organic fractionated coconut oil for the most environmentally friendly option.

RAPESEED WAX

A natural plant wax made from the oil extracted from rapeseed. I use this wax to make my own candles as it burns cleanly and holds scent well. Rapeseed is renewable, sustainable, biodegradable and vegan. It is widely grown in the UK and Europe, so rapeseed wax has a much smaller carbon footprint than imported waxes like soy, coconut or palm. If rapeseed wax is difficult to find, choose a non-GMO soy wax instead. To make container candles (see page 148), you will also need to buy a set of wooden wicks and a pack of wooden wick sustainers (clips that hold the wicks in place).

MELT AND POUR SOAP BASE

Making your own soap bars is easy when you use a melt and pour soap base. There are lots of options available but not all of them are good for the environment. Many contain palm oil or mineral oil (a by-product of petroleum) and others are derived from GMO crops or contain animal fats. I like to use a base that is vegan, non-GMO and free from palm oil and synthetic surfactants. My soap base of choice is made with argan oil as it is rich in vitamin E and very nourishing for skin. I also like to use an oatmeal and shea butter base as it is naturally exfoliating

yet gentle. Both bases work well on their own or they can be scented with essential oils, herbal extracts, poppy seeds or dried flowers from the garden. Search online for local suppliers.

BEESWAX

I buy bars from a local hardware store as they sell 100% English beeswax produced in small batches. Search online for local suppliers or speak to a regional beekeeper's association who may be able to supply you directly. Beeswax pellets are widely available online from soap-making supply stores (choose the organic option if possible). There are vegan alternatives to beeswax, which you can also find online, but be aware that these are made with paraffin wax and therefore are not sustainable.

In the Kitchen

'*The best time for planning a book is when you are doing the dishes.*'

Agatha Christie

In the kitchen

I began my green cleaning journey in the kitchen. I was initially dismayed by all the unnecessary commercial cleaners that I had crammed into a tiny cupboard. Most of these products were never used and bought on a whim, while others had been opened, deemed useless and then relegated to the back of the cupboard.

I decided it was time to make some positive changes and researched alternatives. I started simply, switching to the homemade castile soap spray (see page 74) to wipe work surfaces and the tops of appliances. I was so impressed with the results and the ease of making the product that I looked at other ways to change my cleaning routine. For the sink, I used the quick scouring powder (see page 76) and for a deeper clean, the orange and rosemary soft scrub (see page 118), both of which made my sink gleam. I then moved on to the hob and oven cleaner (see pages 86 and 88). Within six months I had stopped buying any commercial cleaning products and my kitchen was cleaner than it had ever been.

Most kitchen cleaners can be replaced successfully with greener options, but the hardest one to change is dishwashing liquid. Sadly, for most people, homemade dishwashing liquid is simply not as effective as its commercial alternative. If you find the homemade version doesn't work for you, don't despair – look at other ways you can make positive changes to your dishwashing routine. Choose eco-friendly products, buy in bulk or look for a refill store where you can take your own container.

Over the next few pages you'll find the recipes that I have tried and tested, and now use on a weekly basis in my own home.

Multipurpose kitchen spray

Castile soap is naturally antibacterial and antifungal, so it's ideal for sanitizing the kitchen. This multipurpose spray is quick to make and can be used to clean hobs (stovetops), countertops, appliances and sinks. It's also safe to use castile soap on stone or marble surfaces as it's an alkaline and it won't etch the soft stone. You can use this spray unscented or add some essential oils for a natural fragrance. I like to use a combination of tea tree essential oil with lemon essential oil as it gives my kitchen a fresh, clean smell and some added antibacterial power, too (see page 64).

Note that castile soap can react with the minerals in hard water, which cause the soap to biodegrade and leave behind a white residue on shiny surfaces. This doesn't cause any damage, but you may have to rinse the surface a couple of times to clean off the white residue. If you live in a hard-water area, then consider using softened or distilled water instead of tap (faucet) water as this will stop the reaction occurring.

How to make kitchen spray

MAKES 1 BOTTLE
YOU WILL NEED:

» 1-litre (35-oz) spray bottle
(see page 36, but don't
forget to adjust the amount
of ingredients to fit the
bottle you have)
» Tap (faucet) water, or
softened/distilled water if
you live in a hard-water area
» 50ml (3 tablespoons)
organic liquid castile soap
» Essential oils (optional)

1 Fill the spray bottle with the
water until it's approximately
5cm (2in) from the top.

2 Add organic liquid castile
soap (always add the water
before the soap, otherwise
the mixture goes foamy).

HOW TO USE

Spray liberally on to the
surface to be cleaned. Wipe
off with a clean cloth.

Diluting the soap with the
water means you are also
diluting the preservative
contained in the soap, which
reduces the shelf life of the
spray. I find this size of spray
bottle lasts 2–3 weeks before
it starts to go off. You will
be able to tell as it starts to
smell but usually before this
happens I've come to the end
of the bottle. Make up a new
batch and you are ready to
go again.

Scouring powder

LEMON AND THYME

What could be greener than a cleaner that is made with herbs from the garden? Along with the zest of lemon, this scouring powder will clean and sanitize your sink and leave it smelling incredible. This recipe is suitable for stainless steel and ceramic sinks.

This scouring powder can also be used on most surfaces, including cooker hobs. Always do a small patch test as bicarbonate of soda (baking soda) is abrasive and can scratch surfaces.

You may find on certain surfaces that the powder leaves a white film. Spray the affected area with a little distilled white vinegar diluted in water and wipe off.

ALTERNATIVE COMBINATIONS:

» All citrus peels (lemon and lime)

» All dried herbs (lavender, thyme and rosemary)

» Orange peel, dried rosemary and rosemary essential oil

» Dried mint leaves + lemon essential oil

» Add a teaspoon of ground cinnamon or nutmeg

How to make scouring powder

MAKES 1 JAR

WHAT YOU WILL NEED:

» Bowl
» Spoon
» Glass jar with metal lid
   (an old jam jar or nut
   butter jar is ideal)
» Scissors
» Funnel
» 200g (1 cup) bicarbonate
   of soda (baking soda)
» Lemon powder *
» Thyme powder *
» Lemon essential oil
(optional)

1 In a bowl, add the bicarbonate of soda, lemon powder and thyme powder. Mix well.

2 If you want a stronger scent, add a few drops of lemon essential oil and mix again.

3 Pour the mixture into the glass jar.

4 Punch several small holes in the metal lid, using scissors. Attach the lid.

5 Label the jar with a sticker/glass pen.

HOW TO USE

Sprinkle the powder into the sink. Scrub with a sponge or cloth. Rinse well.

* There are no exact measurements for the lemon or thyme powder as these will vary depending on how much herb or citrus peel you have dried. See page 66 for instructions on how to dry and make powders from herbs and citrus fruits.

Blocked drains

Kitchen sinks can often become blocked by bits of food, soap scum, grease and fat. Rather than using an industrial drain cleaner which contains caustic chemicals, there is an easier and greener solution, using boiling water and bicarbonate of soda (baking soda).

I like to use bicarbonate of soda (baking soda) with herb and citrus powder (see page 66) as it leaves behind a fresh, clean aroma, but you could also use a few drops of essential oils or leave it unscented.

If you have a plunger or a drain cleaning wire brush, use these first to try and dislodge any trapped debris.

If slow-draining kitchen or bathroom sinks are a recurring problem in your home, I recommend investing in a set of wooden sink brushes. These usually comprise of a plughole brush, an overflow brush and a hair-catching brush and are ideal for taking care of blockages.

I've included this subject in the Kitchen chapter, but bathroom sinks and tubs can suffer from blocked drains too. In most cases, blockages in the bathroom are caused by loose hair, but soap scum can also be problematic. Follow the same method to clean out the blockage but remove any trapped hair first.

How to make drain cleaner

MAKES 1 JAR

YOU WILL NEED:

» Mixing bowl
» Spoon
» Boiling water
» 90g (½ cup) bicarbonate of soda (baking soda)
» Herb and citrus powder (see page 66)

1 Add the bicarbonate of soda to the mixing bowl. Add the herb and citrus powder, stir to combine, then set aside.

2 Boil the kettle (or a pan of water on the stove).

HOW TO USE

First, remove any debris that may be caught in the plughole. Pour the boiling water down the plughole. Repeat this twice more.

Pour the bicarbonate of soda and citrus powder mix into the plughole and leave for 30 minutes. Flush with boiling water.

The best way to keep your drains free from blockages is to take some preventative measures:

In the kitchen: don't pour any oil, fat or greasy substance down the drain. Once a week, add some bicarbonate of soda to the plughole and leave overnight. In the morning, flush with boiling water.

In the bathroom: when you are cleaning the shower tray or bathtub, wipe any stray hairs away with a cloth rather than flushing them down the plughole. You can also fit filter traps to stop hairs from getting into the drain.

Dishwashing liquid

BASIL, GRAPFRUIT AND PEPPERMINT

Homemade dishwashing liquid is by far the trickiest 'recipe' to get right. There are thousands of versions online and while many people will have positive results using a recipe, others fail miserably with the same formula.

The answer is just to keep experimenting until you find one that works for you. Try the soap nut tea (see page 82), which can also be used for hand washing dishes if the recipe below isn't quite right for you. When you first start using homemade dishwashing liquid, you'll be disappointed by the lack of bubbles. This is because foaming agents are added to commercial cleaning products to create suds. These bubbles don't do any actual cleaning, it's the detergent in the formula that does all the work.

If you live in an area with hard water, you might find that the castile soap used in this recipe leaves a white film on glassware and crockery. This isn't harmful, but it will lead to an increase in water consumption as each dish will need to be rinsed in clean water.

Note: If you handwash dishes, only fill the bowl halfway to conserve water. You can also use the grey water that is left behind after dishwashing to water the garden. If the water is greasy, pour it on the roots of mature shrubs and trees rather than over young plants. Grey water can also be used to feed fruit or vegetable crops, but avoid any parts of the plant that are edible. Allow the water to cool before adding it to a watering can and aim to use it within 24 hours.

How to make diswashing liquid

MAKES 1 BOTTLE

YOU WILL NEED:

» Heatproof mixing bowl
» Spoon
» Glass storage bottle with pump attachment or repurpose an old plastic bottle of commercial dishwashing liquid
» Funnel
» 300ml (1¼ cups) boiling water
» 1 tablespoon soda crystals (washing soda)
» 100ml (½ cup) liquid castile soap
» ½ teaspoon glycerine
» 2 drops basil essential oil
» 4 drops grapefruit essential oil
» 4 drops peppermint essential oil

1 Pour the boiling water into the mixing bowl. Add the soda crystals and stir until they have dissolved.

2 Pour in the liquid castile soap, stir to combine.

3 Add the glycerine, stir to combine, then add the essential oils and stir to combine.

4 Attach the funnel to the top of the glass/plastic bottle. Pour the mixture through the funnel into the bottle.

5 Attach the pump and screw to tighten. Label the bottle.

HOW TO USE

Add two tablespoons per sink of water and hand wash the dishes as normal.

This recipe will form a thick gel as it cools. If it gets too thick, simply add a little hot water and stir to combine.

Soap nut tea

FOR HANDWASHING AND THE DISHWASHER

A good alternative to dishwashing liquid is to use soap nuts. On page 56 you can read all about these magnificent fruit shells and why they are so useful for green cleaning.

Soap nuts work more effectively when they are added to hot water because they release natural saponins contained in the dried shells. Rather than adding a handful to the dishwashing bowl or popping them into the dishwasher, soap nuts perform better when they are boiled and made into a soap nut tea.

I like to add a few drops of lemon and peppermint essential oils to the tea to give it a light fragrance, but they are not necessary.

Note: This recipe also works well as a liquid laundry detergent.

How to make handwash and dishwasher liquid

MAKES 1 BOTTLE

YOU WILL NEED:

» Large saucepan
» Funnel
» Large plastic bottle (a repurposed cordial, milk or soft drinks bottle is ideal)
» 100g (3½oz) soap nuts
» Water
» 4 drops lemon essential oil (optional)
» 4 drops peppermint essential oil (optional)

1 Add the soap nuts to a large saucepan. Cover with 2 litres (2 quarts) of water and bring to the boil.

2 Simmer for 30 minutes, occasionally squeezing the soap nuts with the back of a spoon to release the soap. Leave overnight to cool.

3 Place the funnel over the top of the plastic bottle opening. Place the sieve over the top of the funnel opening and strain the soap nut liquid (compost the spent soap nuts).

4 Add the essential oils to the bottle, if using.

5 Label the bottle.

HOW TO USE

Add 2 tablespoons to hot water. Wash as normal.

How to use in the dishwasher: Fill the soap dispenser with the tea. Run the washing programme as normal.

You can use this recipe for both handwashing dishes and in the dishwasher. However, soap nuts only have a short shelf life. Keep this tea in the fridge where it will last for up to 2 weeks.

Stainless steel cleaner

This is the simplest and most effective way I have found to clean the stainless-steel appliances in my home. Using only two ingredients that you probably already have in the larder – olive oil and vinegar – this recipe cleans grime and removes fingerprints and makes the stainless steel so shiny you can use it as a mirror!

Distilled white vinegar is used to clean and disinfect any surfaces. However, as it is an acid, it's important to remove any trace of it after use as it could react with the metal over time. A quick wipe down with a wet cloth can prevent that from occurring.

If you have already made one of the scented vinegar sprays on page 116, then you can use this in place of the vinegar and water in the recipe opposite.

How to make stainless steel cleaner

**MAKES 1 BOTTLE
YOU WILL NEED:**

» Spray bottle

» Funnel

» Bottle of distilled white
  vinegar (see page 44)

» Water

» 3 dry, clean cloths or rags

» Hand towel or tea towel
  (dish towel)

» Olive oil

1 Use the ratio one part
vinegar to two parts water.
Attach the funnel and pour
the vinegar into the spray
bottle. Top with cold water
from the kitchen tap (faucet)
or distilled water.

2 Label the spray bottle.

HOW TO USE

Spray liberally onto the
stainless-steel surface. Look
closely for the grain direction
and using a clean dry cloth,
wipe the surface following
the direction of the grain.

Once any dirt or fingerprints
are removed, go over the
surface again with a clean
wet cloth to ensure that any
traces of the acid are removed.
Dry the surface with a hand
towel or tea towel as this helps
to prevent water spotting.

Pour a little olive oil onto
the third clean dry cloth and
rub it in to the surface, again
following the direction of
the grain.

Hob cleaner

Whenever I'm wiping down kitchen work surfaces and the tops of appliances, I generally use the multipurpose castile soap (see page 48) as it's good at shifting dirt.

However, if there are tough food stains or grease spots on the cooker hob (stovetop) that are harder to shift, I like to use this cream cleaner made from bicarbonate of soda (baking soda) and liquid castile soap. It cuts through dirt and grease easily, leaving my hob sparkling.

For use on stainless steel, enamel and glass hobs: It's worth investing in a hob-cleaning scraper to remove any tough deposits, sticky marks and burns. Suitable for all types of hob, it is made from metal and won't scratch any delicate surfaces. The hob scraper also comes in handy for cleaning the inside glass on the oven door, tiles and splashbacks. You can find them in kitchenware stores or search online.

How to make hob cleaner

FOR 1 APPLICATION YOU WILL NEED:

» Mixing bowl
» Spoon
» Reusable sponge
» 2 cloths
» 60g (⅓ cup) bicarbonate of soda (baking soda)
» 60ml (4 tablespoons) liquid castile soap

1 Add the bicarbonate of soda to the mixing bowl.

2 Pour the liquid castile soap into the bowl. Stir to combine until the mixture forms a paste. If it's too thick, add a little more liquid castile soap.

HOW TO USE

Dip a reusable sponge into the cleaning paste. Using circular motions, rub the sponge onto the hob (stovetop). Repeat until all the surface is covered with the cleaning paste

Once you have covered all the surface, take a clean, damp cloth and rinse the cleaning paste off. You will have to rinse and wring the cloth out a few times to remove all the cleaning paste from the hob. Wipe over the surface with a dry cloth.

Oven cleaner

The main ingredient in commercial oven cleaners is sodium hydroxide (also known as caustic soda), a substance that is both corrosive and toxic.

Warning labels on the packaging are very clear on the harm these products can do to your wellbeing, including skin burns, eye damage and breathing difficulties.

Cleaning the oven is a horrible job, but it can be done safely and hygienically by using a few natural ingredients and following this method.

Suitable for stainless steel and enamel cookers.

Additional oven tips:

Line the bottom of your oven with a sheet of aluminium foil (preferably recycled, as it uses less energy to produce than regular foil). When it has become grubby, remove the sheet and wash under cold water. Leave to dry, then add to your kerbside recycling. Line the oven with a clean sheet of foil.

Alternatively, place a bowl of water (use a heatproof bowl) in the oven after you have finished using it. Turn up the oven temperature to the hottest setting and leave for ten minutes. This allows the water to steam clean the oven walls and floor. Allow the oven to cool and then wipe everything down with a clean, dry cloth. You could also add a couple of slices of fresh lemon to the bowl of water to help remove any strong odours.

How to make oven cleaner

FOR 1 APPLICATION YOU WILL NEED:

» Glass mixing bowl
» Spoon
» 2 reusable sponges
» 2 cloths
» 60g (⅓ cup) bicarbonate of soda (baking soda)
» 60ml (¼ cup) water
» Vinegar spray (see page 116)

1 Remove any wire racks, trays or thermometers from inside the oven. Wash the wire racks in warm, soapy water and leave to air dry.

2 Add the bicarbonate of soda to the glass mixing bowl. Add the water and stir to form a paste.

HOW TO USE

On the oven walls: Apply a little of the paste to a reusable sponge and rub it over the interior walls of the oven (make sure you avoid any heating elements). Leave overnight.

In the morning, use a damp cloth to rinse off the paste. You may have to rinse the cloth several times to remove all the paste.

Spray the interior walls of the oven with the vinegar spray. Rinse off with a clean, damp cloth

On the glass door: Apply a little of the paste to a reusable sponge and using circular motions, rub it into the door. Leave for 30 minutes. Using a clean damp cloth, rinse off the paste.

Spray with the vinegar mix. Rinse off with a clean, damp cloth. Leave the door open to dry.

Dealing with burnt-on food

Trying to get saucepans, roasting dishes or frying pans (skillets) clean from burnt-on food remnants can be tedious and frustrating work. By harnessing the magic cleaning power of bicarbonate of soda (baking soda), grease spots and encrusted food stains can be easily lifted without the need for heavy scrubbing.

For tough stains on enamel dishes:
Add a tablespoon of bicarbonate of soda to the dish. Squeeze a little liquid castile soap on top of the powder, add a teaspoon of salt and mix with a spoon. Using a damp cloth, rub the paste into the stained areas. Leave for ten minutes and then scrub hard with a scouring pad.

For use on stainless steel/enamel saucepans

FOR 1 APPLICATION YOU WILL NEED:

» Mixing bowl
» Spoon
» Reusable sponge or copper scouring pad
» 50g (¼ cup) bicarbonate of soda (baking soda)
» 125ml (½ cup) hot water

1 Add the bicarbonate of soda to the mixing bowl. Add the hot water and stir to make a paste (if it's too thick, add a little more water than the given amount).

2 Using a reusable sponge or a copper scouring pad, gently scrub the paste into any burnt areas. Repeat until all the paste is used up.

3 Rinse and wash as normal.

For use on roasting dishes

FOR 1 APPLICATION YOU WILL NEED:

» Spatula
» 90g (½ cup) bicarbonate of soda (baking soda)
» 250ml (1 cup) hot water

1 Sprinkle the roasting dish with the bicarbonate of soda. Pour the hot water on to the bicarbonate of soda. Set aside for 1 hour.

2 Scrape the burnt bits and the sides of the dish with a spatula.

3 Empty, wash and rinse the dish in hot, soapy water.

For use on non-stick frying pans (skillets)

FOR 1 APPLICATION YOU WILL NEED:

» Mixing bowl
» Spoon
» 50g (¼ cup) bicarbonate of soda (baking soda)
» 125ml (½ cup) hot water

1 Add the bicarbonate of soda to the mixing bowl. Add the hot water and stir to make a paste (if it's too thick, add a little more water than the given amount or if it's too runny, add extra bicarbonate of soda).

2 Spoon the paste on to the bottom of the frying pan. Set aside for 30 minutes.

3 Rinse and wash as usual.

Cleaning the microwave

This is one of the easiest and most effective ways to clean the microwave. It uses only two ingredients – water and fresh lemon juice. The steam from the water helps to lift off any food remnants and grease spots, while the lemon deodorizes and kills bacteria.

This recipe uses a fresh lemon, cut and squeezed. However, you can also use 2–3 tablespoons of lemon juice for this purpose. This is a good option if you have any frozen lemon juice (defrost first before using) or you have made the citrus peel powder on page 66 and have some leftover juice.

How to make microwave cleaner

FOR 1 APPLICATION YOU WILL NEED:

» Microwave-safe glass bowl
» Clean dishcloth or cotton rag
» Knife
» 250ml (1 cup) water
» 1 lemon

1 Place the water in the bowl.

2 Slice the lemon in half with the knife. Squeeze the juice from the two lemon halves into the water, then add the squeezed lemon halves to the water as well. (If you are using leftover lemon juice, add that to the water in place of the lemon halves.)

HOW TO USE

Remove any debris or crumbs from the microwave first.

Place the bowl containing the water, lemon juice and lemon halves in the microwave. Set for 3 minutes on high power so the water comes to the boil.

Leave the bowl in the microwave for 5 minutes, then remove the bowl from the microwave and set aside (be careful as it may still be hot).

Lift out the turntable and wipe it down with a damp dishcloth or cotton rag. Wipe the inside of the microwave, starting with the ceiling and working your way down the sides to the floor. Wipe the inside of the door. Replace the turntable.

If your microwave is very grubby, you may need to repeat this method two or three times, reusing the same bowl of lemon water. You can also dip your dishcloth or rag into the lemon water and apply it directly to any tough spots that need a little more elbow grease to remove them.

In the Laundry

'*A place for everything, and everything in its place.*'

Mrs Beeton

Laundry

If you are looking to become greener when doing the laundry, one of the best thing you can do is to wash things less often – clothes can usually be worn several times before they need to be laundered. It's also useful to consider the amount of energy and water you consume and look at ways to conserve it. Wait until you have a full load of laundry before you turn the machine on and adjust the temperature to 30°C, as this is the most energy efficient. Regular maintenance of your washing machine also helps to keep it free from bad odours and prevents limescale and mould developing.

Switching to a natural laundry detergent is another way to make a positive impact. There are lots of different recipes online for making your own detergent, but I aim to keep mine simple by using only three key ingredients – Savon de Marseille soap, soda crystals (washing soda) and bicarbonate of soda (baking soda). Together, these three ingredients have the power to clean, soften fabrics and remove tough stains. I also add a few drops of essential oils to the recipe to create a light fragrance.

Ditch the fabric conditioner altogether and use distilled white vinegar to soften fabrics instead (see page 104). If you have any clothing or homeware made from synthetic fibres such as fleece or acrylic, be aware that these release tiny microfibres every time they are washed. Eventually these tiny fibres end up in rivers or the sea where they can enter the food chain and harm aquatic lifeforms. Use a microfibre catching ball or bag every time you wash any synthetic fibres. Reducing the spin cycle when you launder synthetic fibres can help because although faster speeds help fabrics dry quicker, they also shed more microfibres.

Clean your washing machine

KEEPING THE WASHING MACHINE IN GOOD CONDITION ENSURES THAT IT CLEANS LAUNDRY PROPERLY AND EFFICIENTLY.

Bacteria, mould and leftover detergent can build up in the machine over time, passing onto fabrics and making laundry smell unpleasant.

When I used commercial detergents and softeners, I would occasionally find my laundry was impregnated with dark, sticky deposits. These deposits were also lurking in the detergent drawer and entrenched in the door seals. The drum interior was often smelly and this odour would spread to my laundry, too. In order to rid the machine of these problems, I'd have to resort to using a specialized commercial cleaning product which was expensive and laden with toxic chemicals.

I've found a noticeable difference in my machine since switching to my own homemade laundry detergents and softeners. I no longer have thick gooey deposits and the dispenser drawer is gunk-free. My laundry is clean and smells fresh, and there are no bad odours coming from the machine either. By sticking to the routine listed opposite, I find my washing machine is clean and running efficiently.

Note: If you are switching from commercial detergents to homemade ones, you may find you have to run the machine with vinegar several times to ensure that it is completely free from gunk and bacteria.

IN THE DRUM (MONTHLY)

Run the empty machine on the hottest temperature setting, adding 500ml (2 cups) distilled white vinegar to the drum.

CLEAN OUT THE FILTER REGULARLY (MONTHLY)

Remove the filter (be careful this doesn't release any excess water from the machine – put some towels down in front of the filter to mop up any water). Remove any bits of gunk or trapped lint. Wipe down with a clean cloth and replace the filter.

DISPENSER DRAWER (MONTHLY)

Fill a basin with hot water and add some liquid castile soap (see page 48). Remove the dispenser drawer and submerge in the hot soapy water for 10 minutes. Using an old toothbrush, scrub away any dirty residue. Rinse well and air dry.

DISPENSER DRAWER INTERIOR (MONTHLY):

After removing the dispenser drawer, check the interior slot for any residue. Spray a little of the multipurpose castile soap spray (see page 74) and using an old toothbrush, scrub away any gunk. Wipe with a clean, damp cloth and leave to air dry. Replace the dispenser drawer.

INSIDE THE GLASS DOOR AND SEALS (WEEKLY)

Liberally spray with the vinegar spray (see page 116), then wipe off any residue using a clean, damp cloth.

LEAVE THE DOOR OPEN TO DRY. (AFTER EVERY USE)

Leave the door open a little to let air circulate around the drum.

Note: Prevent mould and mildew in the washing machine by leavig the door and drawer open after every wash. Also don't leave recently laundered items in the machine for too long as mould and mildew thrive in warm, damp environments. Remove from the machine and allow them to air dry.

Liquid laundry detergent

ROSE, GERANIUM AND LAVENDER

If you prefer a liquid detergent to a powder one, you may like to give this recipe a try. It washes fabrics well and has good stain-removing properties, but you will find it is much thinner than a commercial liquid detergent. Don't be put off by this – it's simply that these natural formulae are more delicate than their chemical counterparts and they don't thicken in the same way.

Before every wash, give the bottle a quick shake as the ingredients can separate. If you don't shake the mixture, the detergent will not be as effective, and you'll be left with lumpy bits at the bottom of the bottle.

This recipe makes enough liquid detergent for approximately 10–12 washes.

Note: Making your own laundry detergent is easy, but it may not be the right choice for you. You could choose to switch to soap nuts instead (see page 56), which are very effective at cleaning and a good option for zero-waste living. If you want to continue using a commercial detergent, then aim to make changes in other ways, such as buying washing powder in cardboard packages and liquids in bulk or using refill stores where you can fill your own container.

How to make liquid detergent

MAKES 1 BOTTLE

YOU WILL NEED:

» Saucepan

» Heatproof glass mixing bowl

» Spoon

» Funnel

» Storage container with sealable lid (a repurposed clean plastic liquid detergent bottle is ideal)

» 1 litre (1 quart) boiling water

» 50g (2oz) Savon de Marseille soap, grated (or use an equal amount of Savon de Marseille soap flakes)

» 50g (2oz) bicarbonate of soda (baking soda)

» 20g (¾oz) glycerine

» 4 drops each rose and geranium essential oils

» 6 drops lavender essential oils

1 Add the boiling water to the glass mixing bowl.

2 Add the grated Savon de Marseille soap or soap flakes. Stir to combine, making sure the soap fully dissolves in the water.

3 Add the bicarbonate of soda and the glycerine and mix well. Add the essential oils and stir to combine. Allow the liquid to cool.

4 Attach the funnel to the top of the bottle. Pour the cooled liquid into the bottle and seal. Label.

HOW TO USE:

If you have an old laundry dosing cap or ball, measure the amount of liquid you need into that and place in the machine. Use a full cap/ball for dirty loads or half a cap for general washing. Alternatively, add approximately 3–4 tablespoons per load of laundry liquid to the detergent drawer.

Powder detergent

CHAMOMILE, LAVENDER AND ORANGE

I like to use a bar of Savon de Marseille olive oil soap for this powder detergent as it is gentle on fabrics and delivers superb cleaning power, removing both dirt and stains. Read more about this wonderful soap on page 50. This recipe makes enough powder detergent to fill a 750-ml (26-oz) glass storage jar, which is enough for approximately 38 washes, using one tablespoon of powder per laundry load. If you have a larger storage container, feel free to double the ingredient quantities.

An important note: grate the bar of Savon de Marseille finely, otherwise you may end up with big clumpy bits left in the dispenser drawer as the soap will not dissolve properly. If you don't have the time to grate the bar, you can substitute the same quantity of Savon de Marseille soap flakes (which you can buy online, packaged in paper sacks).

This detergent can be used for most fabrics. However, for washing baby clothes, delicate fabrics or woollens, launder with a little Savon de Marseille soap or soap flakes.

Note: There is nothing better than laundry that has been dried outdoors in the sunshine. It's gentler for fabrics and it will save both money and energy.

How to make powder detergent

MAKES 1 JAR

YOU WILL NEED:

- » Glass mixing bowl
- » Spoon
- » Grater
- » Funnel
- » Glass storage jar with lid
- » 250g (9oz) soda crystals (washing soda)
- » 250g (9oz) bicarbonate of soda (baking soda)
- » 250g (9oz) Savon de Marseille olive oil soap (or Savon de Marseille soap flakes)
- » 10 drops roman chamomile essential oil
- » 10 drops lavender essential oil
- » 10 drops orange essential oil

1 Add the soda crystals and the bicarbonate of soda to the glass mixing bowl.

2 Using a handheld grater, finely grate the Savon de Marseille soap. Add the grated soap to the mixing bowl.

3 Add the essential oils. Mix well with the spoon.

4 Attach the funnel to the top of the glass storage jar. Tip the ingredients through the funnel into the jar. Seal and label.

HOW TO USE

Add 1 tablespoon of the powder to the detergent drawer in the washing machine.

Herbal fabric conditioner

Fabric conditioner was a product I used a lot of the time. I liked how soft it made my clothes and towels feel, as well as the fragrance it imparted. But using it regularly can reduce the absorbency of fabrics and prevent laundry detergent from cleaning effectively. Fabric softener can also encourage the growth of mould and bacteria in the washing machine.

There are several environmental issues arising from fabric softener use. Many commercial brands contain ingredients derived from petrochemicals, palm oil and animal fats. Some of these ingredients are not biodegradable and can be harmful to aquatic lifeforms when they are washed down the drain.

If you use fabric softener regularly, there is a simpler, less expensive option – distilled white vinegar.

Before I tried it, I had concerns that my laundry would smell strongly of the vinegar. The opposite is true; there is no smell at all, and the vinegar is great at softening fabrics. Additionally, vinegar cuts through grease build-up, helping to clean your washing machine every time you use it. Below you will find the recipe for a natural fabric conditioner using fresh herbs from the garden. Rosemary, sage and thyme will not colour the vinegar, so won't cause staining. Alternatively, you could add a few drops of your favourite essential oils or use distilled white vinegar on its own as a fabric softener.

If you have hard water, you may find you need to add a little more than the 50ml (2oz) suggested in the recipe to get the best results for your laundry.

How to make fabric conditioner

MAKES 1 BOTTLE

YOU WILL NEED:

» 1-litre (1-quart) glass storage jar

» 1-litre (1-quart) glass bottle with sealable lid

» Funnel

» Sieve

» 1 litre (1 quart) distilled white vinegar

» Handful of fresh herbs (I use rosemary, sage and thyme), washed and dried

1 Place the herbs in the glass storage jar. Pour the bottle of white distilled vinegar over the herbs until they are completely submerged.

2 Seal the jar and place in a dark cupboard for 48 hours.

3 Attach the funnel to the glass bottle. Place the sieve on top of the funnel and strain the vinegar and herb mix. Seal the bottle and label. The leftover herbs can be composted

HOW TO USE

Add 50ml (2oz) of the herb-infused vinegar to the fabric softener dispenser in your washing machine. Wash as normal.

Stain removers

Use this laundry stain removal spray to pre-treat difficult stains like tomato sauce, ink, coffee and red wine. Try to get the stain treated as quickly as possible before it's allowed to set, as leaving it can make it harder to remove. If the stain has set, you may find you have to use the stain removal spray several times.

REMOVING GREASY STAINS ON RUGS OR CARPETS

Deal with grease or oil spills on rugs or carpets immediately to prevent any permanent marks or residue. Blot the stain with a clean tea towel (dish towel) or cloth, but don't rub. Lift the towel or cloth and cover the stain with bicarbonate of soda (baking soda). Leave overnight. In the morning, vacuum up the bicarbonate of soda. There will still be grease in the carpet fibres, which will need to be removed, so cover the stain with a little dishwashing liquid. Use a clean, damp cloth and dab the stain to soak up the remainder of the grease. Blot the stain once more with a clean tea towel or cloth and sprinkle over some more bicarbonate of soda. Leave overnight and in the morning, vacuum the area again.

How to make stain remover

MAKES 1 BOTTLE
YOU WILL NEED:

» 500-ml (16-oz) spray gun (see page 36 and adjust the amount of ingredients to fit the bottle you have)
» 350ml (1½ cups) water from the kitchen tap (faucet)
» 60ml (¼ cup) dishwashing liquid (from the shops or the recipe on page 80)
» 60ml (¼ cup) glycerine

1 Add the dishwashing liquid and the glycerine to the bottle (if using a commercial dishwashing liquid).

2 Top with the water. Shake gently to combine.

HOW TO USE
Spray liberally onto the stain. Leave for 1 hour, then launder as normal.

How to get rid of sweat stains on fabrics

FOR 1 APPLICATION
YOU WILL NEED:

» Glass mixing bowl
» Spoon
» 4 tablespoons bicarbonate of soda (baking soda)
» Warm water

1 Place the bicarbonate of soda in the bowl.

2 Add a little warm water and start stirring. Keep adding the water until you achieve a paste-like consistency.

HOW TO USE
Spoon the paste onto the affected area of the fabric. Rub the fabric together, allowing the paste to absorb into the stain. Leave for 1 hour. Rinse under cold water. Launder as normal.

In the Bathroom

'The power of finding beauty in the humblest things makes home happy and life lovely.'

Louise May Alcott

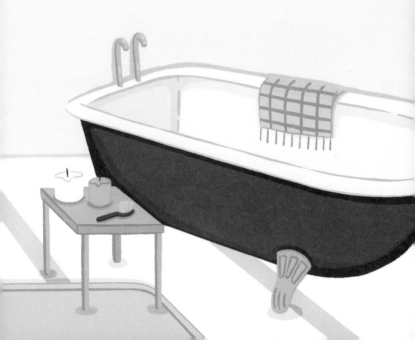

In the bathroom

Keeping your bathroom clean and free from harmful bacteria is crucial and many believe that the answer to the question of keeping us safe lies with bleach. However, there are greener alternatives which work just as effectively. Vinegar (see page 44) and citric acid (see page 52) make an invincible team with their combined disinfecting power and antibacterial properties. Start cleaning in the bathroom with the toilet area. Sprinkle a little citric acid into the toilet bowl the night before you clean because this is key for getting rid of tough mineral deposits and hard-water stains. The following morning, flush to complete the cleaning of the pan, clean the outside of the toilet, the seat and the cistern with the vinegar spray (see page 116).

For sinks, bathtubs and shower areas, use the vinegar spray or opt for the orange and rosemary soft scrub (see page 118), which both freshens and sanitizes. Don't forget that vinegar must not be used on porous surfaces and never at the same time as bleach (see page 25). If you need to tackle any nasty aromas in the bathroom, you can dust a little toilet freshening powder (see page 124) around the rim of the toilet to disinfect and help remove bad odours. If your bathroom has a window, open it and let the fresh air do the work.

Of course, it's not only the toilet and the washing facilities that need looking after in the bathroom. Shower screens and shower curtains are prone to mildew and can harbour nasty bacteria, while tiles and grout are susceptible to mould. Instead of reaching for a toxic cleaning product, take a look at the recipe ideas on page 120 for cleaning the shower curtain and page 122 for dealing with mould on tiles and grout.

Foaming handwash

SAGE, ROSEMARY AND LAVENDER

We used to go through so many plastic bottles of handwash. I bought cheap supermarket own-brand versions and occasionally more expensive brands that came in pretty bottles with exotic sounding ingredients. But regardless of price, the empty bottles were ultimately going to end up in the recycling bin or thrown away to landfill.

The greenest option when it comes to washing your hands is to switch to a bar of natural soap. Many shops are now selling these unpackaged, which helps to further reduce the amount of waste we produce. Alternatively, you can find my recipe for making your own bar soap on page 114. However, sometimes a bar of soap isn't practical. If you have young children, you'll know that handwashing is often haphazard and using a bar of soap may not be effective for keeping little hands clean and safe. It's very simple to make this natural antibacterial handwash to keep handy in the kitchen or bathroom.

I like to use a mixture of essential oils to scent this handwash, but they are optional. If you do have young children, lavender is considered gentle and safe to use, so you could choose to make the handwash with a few drops of lavender essential oil only.

Notes: the mixture may separate, so give it a quick shake to combine. Since oil is added to the mixture, the soap can feel a little greasy when you first use it. The oil is there to nourish the skin, leaving it feeling soft and smooth, but you can reduce the amount of oil added or leave it out altogether.

How to make foaming handwash

**MAKES 1 BOTTLE
YOU WILL NEED:**

» 500-ml (16-oz) glass bottle
with pump dispenser (see
page 36)
» Funnel
» 150ml (⅔ cup) liquid
organic castile soap
» 2 tablespoons organic
fractionated coconut oil
» 1 tablespoon glycerine
» Cooled, boiled water or
distilled water
» 8–10 drops sage essential oil
» 8–10 drops rosemary
essential oil

» 8–10 drops lavender
essential oil

1 Attach the funnel to the
neck of the bottle.
2 Pour the liquid castile soap
into the glass bottle. Add the
fractionated organic coconut
oil and the glycerine.

3 Fill to the top of the glass
bottle with the cooled, boiled
water (or distilled water), then
add the essential oils, one at a
time. Shake gently to combine.

4 Attach the pump and
tightly screw to fix. Label
the bottle.

Lemon and poppy seed soap bar

Soap-making is quick and easy using the 'melt and pour' method. It doesn't require any specialized equipment and it's a great way to get creative in the kitchen. I use the entire 1kg (2oz) bar because that fits my mould but you can reduce the quantities in the recipe for the size of mould you intend to use.

Any item that holds water can be repurposed as a mould for soap making – jelly moulds, muffin tins (pans), yogurt pots or plastic sandwich boxes all work well. I use a silicone loaf tin which can hold 1.2kg (42oz) of soap and this makes 12 bars.

This lemon and poppy seed bar is perfect for using in the bathroom or kitchen. The lemon adds a wonderful freshness and the poppy seeds exfoliate, so you can use this in the shower or bath too. Homemade soap bars make wonderful gifts for family members, friends or teachers. Wrap them in twine and add a handwritten tag with the ingredients on.

VARIATIONS

I like to add some botanical or herbal elements such as dried lavender or rose petals to my soap bars. Gently stir them into the soap along with the essential oils. Alternatively, save a few dried flowers or herbs for the top of your soap bar. Allow the soap to sit for 10 minutes after pouring it into your mould, then sprinkle a few dried flowers or herbs onto the surface. Set aside as before.

How to make a soap bar

MAKES 12 BARS
YOU WILL NEED:

» Large heavy-based saucepan
» Spoon
» Soap mould (see opposite)
» Knife
» 1kg (2lb 2oz) bar melt and pour soap (see page 69)
» 1 organic unwaxed lemon, zested
» 2 tablespoons poppy seeds
» 20 drops lemon essential oil

1 Cut the melt and pour soap bar into chunks and add to the saucepan. Gently heat the saucepan and start to melt the soap (once the soap has fully melted you need to work quickly and add any fragrances or botanical elements).

2 Add the lemon zest, poppy seeds and essential oils. Stir quickly to avoid a skin forming on the surface of the soap.

3 Pour carefully and slowly into the prepared soap mould. Set aside and leave to cool at room temperature for 48 hours.

4 Remove from the mould, or cut into bars if using a silicone loaf tin, and wrap in greaseproof paper.

Geranium Rose and Lavender
» 20 drops geranium rose essential oil
» 20 drops lavender essential oil
» Pinch of dried rose petals

Lavender, Peppermint and Rosemary
» 20 drops lavender essential oil
» 20 drops peppermint essential oil
» 20 drops rosemary essential oil
» Pinch of finely chopped dried flowers and herbs – lavender, peppermint, rosemary (strip the flowers and leaves from the stalk).

Vinegar sprays

This vinegar spray can be used in place of the multipurpose spray on page 74. I prefer to use the castile soap spray for cleaning in the kitchen and use a vinegar spray for the bathroom. The choice is yours, but please remember that vinegar can attack porous surfaces, so needs to be used with caution.

The most common complaint about cleaning with vinegar is its smell. It is pungent, but there are ways to combat this. From adding slices of citrus fruit and herbs from the garden to scenting with essential oils, the secret is to make an infusion.

I've given a few suggestions opposite to help inspire you. No matter which fruits, herbs or oils you choose, the longer you let them infuse the more it lessens the scent of the vinegar. I typically leave fruits, herbs and oils to infuse for 3–4 weeks. After that time,

simply strain the vinegar into a clean jar with a lid and compost the citrus or herbs that are left behind.

FROM THE GARDEN: THYME, SAGE + MINT

Take cuttings from garden herbs or even use packets from the supermarket. If you cut them from the garden, make sure you shake the cuttings as little bugs can be hiding in the leaves. Wash well, then air dry. Pop the cuttings into the glass jar and top with vinegar. Seal and leave to infuse.

FORAGE: PINE + ORANGE

Shake the pine tree cuttings to make sure there is nothing hiding in the needles. Wash well, then air dry. Strip the needles from the branches and add to the glass jar. Wash and dry an orange. Cut into thin slices and add to the jar of pine needles. Top with vinegar. Seal and leave to infuse.

How to make vinegar spray

**MAKES 1 BOTTLE
YOU WILL NEED:**
» Glass container with
   a lid (Kilner jar, Mason
   jar, recycled jam jar,
   coffee jar, etc)
» Spray bottle (see page 36)
» 1 bottle distilled white
   vinegar (see page 44)
» Water or distilled water
» Essential oils (optional),
» Herbs (optional)
» Citrus slices – oranges,
   lemons, limes, grapefruit,
   etc (optional)

1 Use a mixture – lemon,
lavender and peppermint.
Wash and dry one lemon.

2 Cut into thin slices and
add to the glass jar. Add a
few drops of lavender and
peppermint essential oils.

3 Top with the vinegar.
Seal and leave to infuse.

TO MAKE THE SPRAY
Use the ratio one part vinegar
to two parts water for the size
of your bottle.

Pour the strained, infused
vinegar into a glass spray
bottle using the ratio above
as a guide. Top with tap
(faucet) water or distilled
water. Label the spray bottle
with your ingredients.

TO USE
Spray onto toilet bowl, rim,
seat and cistern. Wipe clean
with a damp cloth. This is a
multi-purpose spray that can
be used to clean countertops,
tabletops etc but must not be
used on any porous surfaces.

Soft scrub

ORANGE AND ROSEMARY

This is my favourite cleaning recipe. I never get tired of making it with its intoxicating aroma and I love how my sink and bathtub sparkle after I've used it. This scrub is highly effective at cutting through soap scum and it's safe to use on plastic and ceramic bathtubs. It can also be used on kitchen sinks and draining boards if you need something stronger than the scouring powder recipe on page 76. This scrub can be used on ceramic, stainless steel and enamel.

The glycerine works here as a natural preservative to lengthen the shelf life of the scrub, usually to around 2 weeks. You may find that the glycerine makes the mixture split, so vigorously shake the jar or stir the mixture with a spoon to combine the ingredients before use. If you are going to make the scrub and use all of it straightaway, feel free to omit the glycerine as it's not essential.

How to make a soft scrub

MAKES 1 JAR
YOU WILL NEED:

» 500g (1lb 2oz) glass
  container with lid
» Glass mixing bowl
» Spoon
» Funnel
» 200g (1 cup) bicarbonate
  of soda (baking soda)
» Pinch of sea salt
» Organic liquid castile soap
  (no precise measurement,
  see instructions below)
» 6 drops rosemary essential oil
» 6 drops orange essential oil
» 1 teaspoon glycerine

1 Add the bicarbonate of soda
and salt to the mixing bowl.

2 Start adding the liquid
castile soap and stir to
combine. There is no
precise measurement for
the castile soap. The ratio is
approximately one third to
one half the measurement
of the bicarbonate of soda,
but you need to add enough
for the mixture to achieve
a paste-like consistency.

3 Add essential oils and the
glycerine. Stir the mixture
until it is well combined.

4 Attach the funnel to the
glass storage jar and pour the
mixture into the funnel. When
the storage jar is full, seal and
label the jar.

HOW TO USE
Pour a little of the paste onto
the surface to be cleaned.
Using a slightly damp reusable
sponge, scrub the mixture onto
the surface. Rinse well with
a clean cloth. Stand back and
admire your shiny sink.

Shower curtain cleaner

Shower curtains can easily become grubby, and are prone to mould and mildew, which can be difficult to get out of the fabric once they take hold. And when they get too dirty, we end up throwing them away, resulting in more waste and the necessity of having to purchase a new shower curtain. There are some simple ways to take better care of a shower curtain and help prolong its lifespan.

After every shower, avoid leaving the curtain bunched up as this helps mildew to develop. Instead, pull the shower curtain fully open and let it dry thoroughly. Mould thrives in humid and moist conditions, so if you can, open a window to air the room immediately after showering. See page 140 for tips on tackling mould and mildew.

If you have an extractor fan instead of a window, leave it running for 5 minutes after you have taken a shower to help remove any excess moisture in the air.

Bicarbonate of soda (baking soda) can be used in the washing machine to freshen a shower curtain and help prevent mildew problems. Pour 50ml

YOU WILL NEED:

» 50g (¼ cup) or 100g (½ cup) bicarbonate of soda (baking soda), depending on how dirty the curtain is
» 50ml (3 tablespoons) organic liquid castile soap
» Distilled white vinegar (enough to fill the fabric softener drawer in your washing machine)

(3 tablespoons) organic liquid castile soap into the detergent drawer and add some distilled white vinegar to the fabric softener drawer. Place 50g (¼ cup) bicarbonate of soda in the washing machine drum along with the shower curtain. Read the washing label carefully to make sure you are using the right temperature and settings required for the fabric before you run the programme.

If the mould or mildew is bad, take the shower curtain down and soak overnight in a solution of warm water with 100g (½ cup) bicarbonate of soda (baking soda). You can do this in a bucket or in a bathtub, just make sure the shower curtain is submerged in the solution. The next day, pop the shower curtain in the washing machine and add 50ml (3 tablespoons) organic liquid castile soap

to the detergent drawer. You can also add some distilled white vinegar to the fabric softener drawer which will help to disinfect and prevent wrinkling. Wash as before.

Air dry the clean shower curtain outside in the sunshine or re-hang in the bathroom and pull fully open to dry.

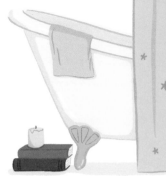

Tile and grout cleaner

Getting grout clean is always tricky. Before I started using natural products, I resorted to scrubbing the white grout with an old plastic toothbrush dowsed in bleach. While this was effective, I was never happy using a product that causes harm to the environment and the wellbeing of my family.

Now I make a paste from three simple ingredients: soda crystals (washing soda), bicarbonate of soda (baking soda) and warm water. The soda crystals cut through dirt and stains, the bicarbonate of soda helps to whiten the grout and combat mould, and the warm water simply binds them together to make a paste. I also add a few drops of tea tree oil and lemon oil as they have natural antibacterial properties, however these are optional.

If you have very grubby grouting, it may take you a few attempts to get the grouting clean. This job also requires some elbow grease, so be prepared to get stuck in and work up a bit of a sweat.

The cleaning paste is more effective when you use a proper grout and tile brush (see page 31) to apply it as the long, hard bristles can get deep into the grouting. You can use an old toothbrush for this job, but as it does not have the abrasive power of the grouting brush, it may not be as successful.

How to make tile and grout cleaner

FOR 1 APPLICATION YOU WILL NEED:

» Glass mixing bowl

» Spoon

» Grout and tile brush

» 100g (4oz) soda crystals (washing soda)

» 100g (½ cup) bicarbonate of soda (baking soda)

» Warm water

» 2 drops tea tree essential oil (optional)

» 2 drops lemon essential oil (optional)

1 Place the soda crystals and bicarbonate of soda in the bowl. Mix together with the spoon.

2 Add a little warm water and stir to combine. You want enough water to make a paste. If it's too runny, simply add more soda crystals to achieve the right consistency.

3 Add two drops of each essential oil if using. Stir to combine.

TO USE

Dab a little of the paste on to the hard bristles of the grouting brush. Scrub the grout thoroughly, reapplying the paste between each tile. Leave for 30 minutes, then rinse off with warm water.

Toilet bowl freshener

Have you ever looked closely underneath the rim of your toilet? You may find some unpleasant brown stains and smells lurking there. I was surprised how revolting my toilet was because I regularly used a green commercial cleaner with a nozzle to clean under the rim. There were lots of brown stains and after some research I discovered this was due to limescale and other mineral deposits. Most commercial cleaning products do contain the ingredients necessary to reduce limescale and mineral deposits, but they don't remove them.

When you search online for recipes to clean your toilet, many of them suggest making toilet 'bombs' from a combination of citric acid and bicarbonate of soda (baking soda). These bombs are made from the same ingredients that you would find in a fizzy bath bomb and they effectively work the same way – the bomb hits the water, it fizzes up and a foam ensues. However, these bombs for cleaning don't really get rid of limescale. To get grubby stains out of the toilet and to clear bad odours, you need to use citric acid on its own and scrub the offending area with an old toothbrush.

I make up a jar of toilet bowl cleaner using citric acid and grapefruit peel powder (see page 66). Together, these ingredients will get rid of tough stains, clear limescale and mineral deposits and leave your toilet smelling fresh and clean. You can even boost the scent of the grapefruit with some grapefruit essential oil if you prefer a stronger fragrance. I use this powder once a week.

How to make toilet bowl freshener

MAKES 1 JAR
YOU WILL NEED:

» Glass bowl
» Spoon
» Funnel
» Glass storage jar with sealable lid
» Old toothbrush
» 200g (1 cup) citric acid
» Grapefruit powder (no precise measurement, see page 66)
» Grapefruit essential oil (optional)

1 Add the citric acid and the grapefruit peel powder to the glass bowl and mix well. Add in a few drops of grapefruit essential oil if you wish.

2 Attach the funnel to the top of the glass storage jar, then pour the powder through the funnel into the jar.

3 Seal with the lid and label the jar.

HOW TO USE
Pour a little of the powder into a glass bowl and dip the toothbrush into the powder. Scrub lightly with the toothbrush under the rim of the toilet. Repeat all the way around the rim. Leave for 5 minutes before flushing.

Other Areas
of the Home

'The true secret of happiness lies in
taking a general interest in all the
details of daily life.'

William Morris

Other areas of the home

This chapter focuses on all those other areas in the home that we need to clean. From wooden flooring and carpets to polishing furniture, there is a simple and natural solution at hand.

Mould and mildew are a persistent problem for many households, and it can be difficult to shift these without resorting to strong chemical cleaning products. These store-bought products normally contain bleach, which can be harmful to wellbeing, causing respiratory problems, sore throats, skin irritation and headaches. Pets are particularly susceptible to bleach in the home and inhalation alone can lead to significant health issues. Bleach can also react with other minerals in water to create dangerous substances, which can cause harm to aquatic lifeforms and take years to decay. However, it is possible to get rid of mould and mildew without using bleach. It just takes a bit of time and elbow grease – see page 140 for my mould removal spray, plus some helpful ideas to prevent it from returning.

Dusting is one of my least favourite tasks, but I know it's vital as I suffer from dust mite allergies. Dust mites thrive in warm, humid environments and live off skin cells shed by humans. Regular dusting helps to deter them, along with the use of certain essential oils like peppermint, sage, lemon and lavender. Rather than turning to disposable dusting wipes or cloths which are synthetically fragranced and ultimately end up in landfill, I like to repurpose old holey socks into lemon and sage-scented dusters (see page 132).

Taking care of carpets and rugs

Carpets and rugs receive a daily battering from feet, pets and outside dirt. Over time, trapped particles that have evaded the vacuum cleaner start to smell unpleasant. Using a carpet and rug freshening powder can neutralize lingering odours and leave your home smelling fresh and clean. This freshening powder can also be used to prevent dust mites taking up residence in a rug or carpet. Dust mites thrive in moist areas, so use this dry powder and vacuum regularly to remove any mites. You can also add six drops of peppermint essential oil to the basic recipe since dust mites are repulsed by its scent.

If you are using this powder to eliminate pet odours, please check with your veterinarian before using any essential oils. As the bicarbonate of soda (baking soda) is the primary deodorizing property in this recipe, you can simply use it on its own.

This powder can also be used in the car to freshen up mats and upholstery.

How to make freshening powder

FOR 1 APPLICATION YOU WILL NEED:

» Glass mixing bowl
» Spoon
» 180g (¾ cup) bicarbonate of soda (baking soda)
» 6 drops citrus essential oil (grapefruit, lemon or orange)
» 6 drops lavender essential oil

1 Add the bicarbonate of soda to the glass mixing bowl.
2 Add the essential oils and stir to combine, removing any lumps.

HOW TO USE

Sprinkle over carpets and rugs and leave for 1 hour or overnight for best results. Then vacuum the carpet or rug to remove the powder.

Sock dusting wipes

LEMON AND SAGE

Disposable wipes for dusting and cleaning have become hugely popular in recent years because they are convenient and easy to use. However, they are not recyclable or biodegradable and will end up sitting in landfill for years. Most of them are infused with toxic chemicals, which can increase indoor air pollution, too. It's simple to make the switch from disposable dusting wipes to ecofriendly reusable options. Cotton socks that have come to the end of their lifespan are perfect to use for reusable dusting wipes. They are quick and easy to use as you can pop one over the top of a rubber glove and run your hand over a surface. You can also repurpose any odd socks that have lost their partners or, alternatively, cut up squares of old cotton t-shirts, sheets or tea towels (dish towels).

These lemon and sage dusting wipes use a little olive oil in the recipe. Choose a light-coloured oil to prevent any staining. The wipes pick up dirt easily without leaving any greasy marks behind and they will gently polish wood too.

Finally, don't forget about looking after houseplants because they need to be regularly dusted and cleaned too. Avoid using the scented dusting socks for plants because the oils can block pores, preventing the plant from breathing properly. On larger houseplants, wipe leaves with a clean, slightly damp cloth. For smaller plants, use a clean bamboo toothbrush and stroke the leaf from the base to the tip to remove any dust. Houseplants also like to have an occasional shower – use lukewarm water and let them air-dry outside in the sun.

How to make dusting wipes

**MAKES 2 WIPES
YOU WILL NEED:**

» Mixing bowl
» Spoon
» Container with lid – glass
  or plastic (I repurposed an
  ice-cream tub)
» Cotton socks or cotton rags
» 250ml (1 cup) hot water
» 2 tablespoons olive oil
» 6 drops lemon essential oil
» 6 drops sage essential oil

1 Add the hot water to the
mixing bowl. Add the olive
oil and essential oils. Stir
to combine.

2 Add the socks or rags one
at a time and coat them in
the oil mix.

3 Squeeze the sock or rags,
then hang to dry (if you are
hanging indoors, put some
cloths or an old towel down
to catch any oil drips).

4 Once the socks or rags
are completely dry, roll
them up and store them
in the container.

HOW TO USE
Use to dust wood,
mantelpieces, lighting, etc.
Once you have finished
dusting, rinse the dusting sock
or rag in cold water and add
it to the laundry pile. Wash
in the machine with other
cleaning cloths, then repeat
the method to make more
dusting socks or rags.

Floor cleaners

I loathe washing floors and will avoid doing them for as long as possible. I much prefer sweeping floors, but eventually the muck gets too obvious to ignore and I reluctantly fetch the mop and bucket.

There are two ways to clean floors naturally. One is using a spray cleaner and the other is the more traditional way with a cotton-headed mop and bucket. The choice of which to use is entirely up to you. I find the spray cleaner handy for getting rid of small areas of grime on flooring and use the mop and bucket method when the floors need a deeper clean.

These cleaners are suitable for most laminate, vinyl and tile flooring. Avoid leaving excess water on laminate as it can damage the surface. Always read the manufacturer's guide to your flooring before using any cleaning product on it and do a small test in an inconspicuous area to make sure it's suitable for your flooring. Make the recipe without essential oils if you have pets in the home.

How to make floor cleaner

Lemon and pine castile soap floor cleaner

FOR 1 APPLICATION YOU WILL NEED:

» Bucket with conical wringer
» Cotton-headed mop
» Dry cloth or tea towel (dish towel)
» 1 litre (1 quart) warm water
» 60ml (¼ cup) liquid castile soap
» 5 drops pine essential oil
» 5 drops lemon essential oil

Add the warm water to the bucket, pour in the liquid castile soap and add the essential oils.

HOW TO USE
Submerge the mop head in the water, then place in the conical wringer and twist to release excess water. Wipe the floor with the mop head using forward and backward strokes, repeating until all the floor has been mopped. Wipe up any excess water from the floor with a clean cloth.

Vinegar spray cleaner

MAKES 1 BOTTLE YOU WILL NEED:

» 1-litre (35-oz) spray bottle (see page 36)
» 500ml (2 cups) warm water
» 125ml (½ cup) distilled white vinegar
» 5 drops lemon essential oil
» 5 drops pine essential oil

1 Add the warm water to the spray bottle, then add the distilled white vinegar and essential oils to the bottle.

2 Shake gently to combine.

HOW TO USE
Spray an area of flooring then wipe over the area with a damp cloth.

Natural beeswax wood polish

This natural beeswax and lemon wood polish nourishes and protects wooden furniture. It uses two main ingredients – olive oil and beeswax – and together they will make your wood shine and highlight the natural beauty of the grain. I have also added a few drops of lemon essential oil for a light fragrance, but you could omit it if you prefer. This polish is suitable to use on most wood surfaces, but is not to be used on wooden floors. It is also safe to use on wooden kitchen utensils and chopping boards.

The measurements for the recipe below make approximately 750ml (3¼ cups) of polish which can fill one large glass container or several smaller recycled jars. This wood polish will stay fresh until the olive oil reaches its expiration date, so check the date printed on your olive oil bottle before making this recipe or if you are buying new, look for a bottle with a long shelf life.

This wood polish makes a nice gift for teachers or to add to Christmas hampers. Make sure to label the jar with the ingredients and instructions for use, as well as the expiration date.

How to make beeswax and lemon wood polish

FOR 1 APPLICATION YOU WILL NEED:

» Heatproof glass mixing bowl

» Saucepan

» Spoon

» Funnel

» Glass storage jar/s (either a 1-litre/35-oz jar or several recycled jam jars/pickle jars etc) with lids

» 150g (⅔ cup) beeswax bar (grated) or pellets

» 600ml (2½ cups) olive oil

» 30 drops lemon essential oil

1 Add the grated beeswax or beeswax pellets to the mixing bowl. Add the olive oil and stir to combine.

2 Fill the saucepan with 5–7.5cm (2–3in) of water and place on the stove. Bring to boil point, then turn the heat down to a gentle simmer.

3 Place the glass bowl over the top of the saucepan, making sure that the base of the bowl does not touch the water in the pan. Let the beeswax melt slowly, stirring occasionally.

4 Once it has fully melted, add the lemon essential oil and stir.

5 Attach the funnel to the jar and pour in the mixture. Label the jar. Allow to cool completely before using.

HOW TO USE
Make sure the area you are going to polish is free from dust. Dab a little of the polish onto a clean cloth and using a circular motion, buff the polish into the grain of the wood. Leave for a few minutes then buff again with a clean cloth.

Windows

Vinegar is a wonderful ingredient for cleaning glass. It quickly breaks down any dirt and film that accumulates on windows, leaving them smudge- and streak-free. I like to use a handheld squeegee to clean my windows as it makes the job far easier. However, if you don't have a squeegee, you can use a damp cloth or an old newspaper. Newspapers are made of dense fibres that don't scratch or leave behind lint.

Be aware that if you are using newspapers the print from ink can leave a mark when it gets wet and this is particularly noticeable on white plastic window frames. The recipe opposite can be used on mirrors, oven doors and glass picture frames. If you are using it on smaller items, like hand mirrors or picture frames, it's better to spray the mix on to a cloth rather than directly on to the surface of an object. Simply wipe the glass with the cloth that has been sprayed with the vinegar mix and dry with a clean cloth.

How to make window cleaner

MAKES 1 BOTTLE
YOU WILL NEED:

» 1-litre (35-oz) spray bottle
(see page 36)

» Slightly damp cotton cloth

» Squeegee

» Old newspaper or dry
cotton cloth

» 250ml (1 cup) distilled
white vinegar

» Water

» Essential oils, such as lemon,
orange and tea tree (optional)

1 Add the distilled white
vinegar to the spray bottle.

2 Fill with 500ml (2 cups)
water and add 3 drops of each
essential oil, if using. Shake to
mix well.

HOW TO USE
Starting at the top of the
window and working from
left to right, spray the vinegar
mix on to the window. Use a
squeegee or cotton cloth and
wipe downward. Move to the
middle half of the window and
repeat as above. Go over the
areas you have wiped with
a clean dry cloth.

Alternatively, starting at
the top of the window and
working from left to right,
spray the vinegar mix on to
the window. Scrunch some
newspaper into a ball and
using circular motions, wipe
the sprayed area. Move to the
middle half of the window and
repeat as above. Add the used
newspaper to the compost bin.

Mould and mildew

Many homes can suffer from mould and mildew problems due to poor ventilation and high humidity levels. Mould thrives in dark, moist conditions, saturating walls and furniture with black or white spores. Mould and mildew can harm your wellbeing and trigger breathing difficulties for those suffering with asthma or allergies.

Lots of people use bleach to try and get rid of mould, but all the bleach does is remove the colour, leaving the spores behind. If you do have mould or mildew on the walls in your home, I've found this spray to be the most effective at getting rid of it. Be careful when using this spray on painted walls or surfaces as some paints can be damaged when they get wet. Always test an inconspicuous area first before use.

Tea tree mould spray

**MAKES 1 BOTTLE
YOU WILL NEED:**

» 1-litre (35-oz) spray bottle (see page 36. If you use a smaller bottle, adjust the quantities below)
» 1 cloth
» 500ml (2 cups) water
» 2 teaspoons tea tree essential oil

1 Add the water to the spray bottle, then add the tea tree essential oil.

2 Attach the spray pump and tighten. Label the bottle.

HOW TO USE
Spray the solution directly onto the mould and leave for 1 hour. Using a slightly damp cloth, wipe over the area and allow to air dry.

Once you have eradicated mould and mildew from your home, try these prevention tips to stop it from reoccurring:

» Open windows to allow fresh air to circulate.
» After a shower or bath, open a window.
» Leave extractor fans running for 10 minutes after showering or having a bath.
» Dry wet areas immediately.

» Use a squeegee to remove condensation from windows and doors.
» Dry washing outdoors rather than indoors.
» Invest in a dehumidifier. These reduce humidity levels, making your home less hospitable to mould and mildew spores. They also remove musty odours that arise from mould and mildew.
» Pop a peace lily in rooms where mould and mildew are a problem. Peace lilies can reduce the amount of mould spores in the air, using them as a food source and absorbing the spores through their leaves. Peace lilies thrive in rooms with high humidity, so bathrooms are ideal.

Scenting the
Home Naturally

*'Live simple, love well, and take time
to smell the flowers along the way.'*

Mark Twain

Scenting the home naturally

If lingering odours from cooking have you reaching for an air freshener, consider the impact this has on the environment and your wellbeing before using one. The majority of air fresheners are manufactured abroad and shipped halfway around the world. Many are made from plastic derived from petroleum and need vast amounts of energy and water to produce. Most air fresheners release volatile organic compounds (VOCs) into the air in your home and can cause respiratory problems, headaches, allergies and asthma. They are also particularly harmful to pets, who can ingest pollutant particles that have settled on their fur when they groom themselves. The good news is there are other ways to scent your home and in this chapter you will find recipes for natural air fresheners that are safe and better for the planet.

I was horrified when I discovered the damage that scented candles can do to the environment. Most are made from paraffin wax (also known as mineral wax) and are a by-product of the petroleum industry. The candles are bleached, artificially dyed and synthetically fragranced and, when they burn, the fumes released are comparable with those of a diesel engine. If you like to use scented candles or give them as gifts, get creative at home and make your own using sustainable plant waxes. On page 148 you'll find the instructions for making grapefruit and lemon container candles using recycled jam jars and vintage teacups.

However, the best way to scent your home is to open a window and let the fresh air in. This helps to counteract indoor air pollution, reduce condensation and release trapped odours. Try to open a window for an hour every day.

Dried herb garland

I grow a lot of fresh herbs in the garden. Some are for use in cooking, others for feeding pollinators, but most I grow purely for their wonderful scents. At the end of the growing season I like to cut and dry them in bunches, along with a few flowers such as alliums, hydrangeas and yarrow. Hung over a window or strung on a piece of twine over the mantelpiece, they not only look beautiful but also retain their intoxicating aromas. Many dried herbs have the added benefit of repelling insects and dust mites, too.

There are no set rules for how many bunches to attach to your garland and please don't feel that you must buy or grow all these herbs to get the benefit of the scent. Lavender on its own would work equally well, and you could forage in the woods for dried grasses, teasels or poppy seedheads if you want to get creative. The flowers and herbs will fade over time, but I think this just adds to their beauty.

Please be aware that it's essential to remove any lower leaves or flowers from stems before you bind them with twine, otherwise they can become mouldy and affect the rest of the bunch.

How to make a herb garland

MAKES 1 GARLAND
YOU WILL NEED:

» Bunches of herbs such as bay leaves, chamomile, lavender, mint, rosemary and/or thyme

» Scissors

» Twine (hemp, jute or sisal are the eco-friendliest)

» Measuring tape

» Pencil

» 2 screw-in hooks or nails

» Hammer

1 Cut the stems of each herb bunch to your chosen length. Strip away any of the lower leaves where you plan to tie the bundles.

2 Cut a 30-cm (12-in) length of twine for each herb bundle. Wrap the twine tightly around the stem of each bundle and secure with a tight knot, leaving one end of the twine long enough to attach to the wall or window.

3 Choose the wall or window where you are going to attach the garland. Using a pencil, lightly mark the spot where each hook or nail will be placed. If you are using hooks, screw these into the wall. If you are using nails, lightly tap them into the wall with the hammer.

4 Cut a piece of twine wide enough to span the wall/window between the fixings, plus an extra 5cm (2in) for tying to the wall fixings.

5 Attach the twine to the fixings securely.

6 Tie each herb bundle to the twine so that they hang down, either all at the same length or vary them to make things more interesting.

Candles

GRAPEFRUIT AND LEMON

These scented candles are some of my favourite things to make. They will leave your home smelling incredible and they are fantastic gifts for friends, family or teachers. In the UK and the EU, rapeseed wax is the most sustainable option for making these candles as it has the lowest carbon footprint. If you can't find rapeseed wax, opt for non-GMO soy wax instead. Both rapeseed and soy wax are vegan, burn cleanly and hold scent well. You can use lots of different items to make container candles, but whatever you choose must not leak, break or catch fire. I like to repurpose old glass candle containers, tin cans, vintage teacups and jam jars. It's difficult to estimate how much wax will fill each container so prepare a few extra ones in advance in case you need them.

Change up the scents with the seasons – in spring, I like to add some herbal scents like sage or rosemary. In winter, I blend citrus scents with eucalyptus or pine oils. For a great Christmas present idea, wrap a piece of twine around the container, add a recycled paper tag and a tiny evergreen sprig.

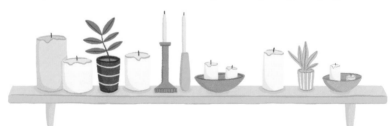

How to make a candle

MAKES 4 CANDLES
YOU WILL NEED:

» Wood wicks

» Metal sustainers

» Containers for candles

» Chopsticks or lolly
(popsicle) sticks

» Clothes pegs (clothes pins)

» Small saucepan

» Heatproof glass mixing bowl

» 500g (1lb 2oz) rapeseed wax
(or soy wax), container blend

» 20 drops grapefruit essential
oil

» 20 drops lemon essential oil

1 Insert a wood wick into a
metal sustainer, then place
the sustainer in the bottom
centre of the container.

2 Lay the chopsticks on top
of the container, either side
of the wood wick and clamp
together with a clothes peg.

This supports the wood wick
and prevents it moving when
wax is added to the container.

3 Break the rapeseed wax into
small pieces and add it to the
glass mixing bowl.

4 Fill the saucepan with water
to a depth of 5–7.5cm (2–3in)
and place on the stove. Bring
the water to the boil, then turn
the heat down to a simmer.

5 Place the glass bowl over the
saucepan, making sure that
the base of the bowl does not
touch the water. Let the wax
melt slowly. Once it has fully
melted, add the essential oils.

6 Pour into the prepared
containers. Leave to set for
approximately 3–4 hours.

7 Remove the chopsticks.
Using a pair of scissors,
trim the wick approximately
1–2cm (½–¾in) above
the candle wax.

Herb sachets

LAVENDER AND PEPPERMINT

These natural herb sachets make your fabrics smell amazing and can help to discourage moths from taking up residence in your home. Moths like to feast on natural fibres like cotton, linen or wool, so pop one of these lavender and peppermint sachets into an area where there is evidence of moth activity as they loathe the smell.

Dust mites thrive in warm, moist conditions and can usually be found living in mattresses and bedding. Like moths, dust mites are repulsed by the powerful scent of lavender and peppermint, so add one or two of these sachets in between a mattress and a mattress protector.

I make these sachets once a year, composting the previous year's contents. I repurpose the muslin bags, giving them a quick wash before I refill them with freshly scented flowers, herbs and essential oils (see page 67 for information on drying herbs). You can buy organic cotton or muslin drawstring bags from craft stores or online, where they are often listed as refillable tea bags or spice bags.

These sachets are ideal for hanging in closets, laundry baskets and chests of drawers. Keep out of the reach of babies, children and pets.

How to make herb sachets

MAKES 6 SACHETS
YOU WILL NEED:

» Glass mixing bowl
» Chopping board
» Knife
» Spoon
» Organic cotton/muslin
  drawstring bags, or muslin
  sheet cut into squares
» 1 bunch dried lavender
» 1 bunch dried peppermint (or
  garden mint, spearmint, etc)
» 10 drops lavender essential oil
» 10 drops peppermint
  essential oil

1 Strip the flower buds from
the dried lavender and add to
the glass mixing bowl.

2 Strip the leaves from the
dried peppermint, place the
leaves on the chopping board
and finely chop with a knife.
Add to the glass mixing bowl
and stir to combine.

3 Add the lavender and
peppermint essential oils and
stir to combine.

4 Fill the cotton/muslin bags
with the mixture.

5 Alternatively, lay down
a muslin square and put a
tablespoon of the mixture
in the middle of the square.
Fold one corner of the square
into the centre of the square
and pull the opposite corner
towards it. Tie both corners
of fabric together. Repeat with
the remaining two corners to
form a bag.

Air fresheners

I used to buy synthetic scented air fresheners made from plastic and had one for every room in my home. Eventually, their smell would fade and because they weren't recyclable, they ended up in landfill. Now, I make my own using repurposed food jars and bicarbonate of soda (baking soda). These natural air fresheners work just as well as the commercial counterparts, with the bonus that once the scent starts to fade you can just top it up with some more essential oils. Pop one of these natural air fresheners wherever you need to in your home, but keep them out of the reach of young children or pets.

You can make these natural air fresheners with herbs and flowers from the garden or just add a few drops of your favourite essential oils. I utilize old jam jars, olive jars or pickle jars as containers, along with their lids. Alternatively, you can attach a piece of muslin cloth over the top of the jar and tie it on with some twine.

Start with the basic ingredient of bicarbonate of soda and add dried herbs, flowers or citrus peel. The dried ingredients will add a subtle yet natural perfume but if you'd like a stronger fragrance, add 5 drops of your chosen essential oil blends. See pages 66 and 67 for instructions on drying herbs and flowers and making citrus peel powders. There are no exact measurements for the dried ingredients, as it's up to you how much you want to add to the mix.

How to make air freshener

MAKES 1 JAR
YOU WILL NEED:

» Glass jar with metal lid

» Scissors or a sharp knife

» Glass mixing bowl

» Spoon

» Funnel

» 360g (2 cups) bicarbonate of soda (baking soda)

» Dried citrus peel powder + grapefruit, lemon and orange essential oils

» Dried herb powder + rosemary and sage essential oils

» Dried lavender + lavender, lemon and rosemary essential oils

» Dried rose petals + geranium rose, grapefruit and lavender essential oils

1 Punch 4–6 holes in the top of your jar lid using a pair of scissors or a sharp knife (watch your fingers!).

2 Add the bicarbonate of soda to the glass mixing bowl. Add the dried ingredients of your choosing to the glass mixing bowl and stir to combine.

3 Add the essential oils (5 drops of each oil) and stir.

4 Attach the funnel to the top of your glass jar and pour the powder into the jar.

5 Screw on the lid.

Room spray

GERANIUM, ROSE, GRAPEFRUIT AND LAVENDER

I always keep a batch of this room spray handy in the cupboard in case I want to do a quick spritz before guests arrive. It's also good for refreshing fabrics or shopping baskets that can get a little smelly after I've used them for grocery shopping.

This room spray can be spritzed in the air, on cushions (pillows), bed linen, sofas or curtains. Always do a patch test on an inconspicuous area before using on any fabric. Vodka is an important ingredient in this recipe. Its main purpose is to disperse the essential oils in the water, but it also acts as a natural preservative. Shake the bottle before you use it to ensure that the essential oils distribute evenly throughout the liquid.

My favourite blend of oils for this spray is geranium rose, grapefruit and lavender because they remind me of the garden in springtime. Feel free to blend your own oils or make seasonal versions with warming herbs and citrus combinations of rosemary, orange and pine oils in the winter months.

Note: You can also scent your home using flowers and plants. Fill vases with scented flowers from the florist or the garden. Wherever possible, choose flowers that are in season and grown locally because these will have a lower carbon footprint. Gather seasonal evergreen branches, bunches of cow parsley or heads of lilac, which smell incredible. If you are foraging, remember to pick responsibly, taking only what you need and seeking permission if you are on private land.

How to make room spray

MAKES 1 BOTTLE
YOU WILL NEED:

» 125-ml (4-oz) spray bottle
  (see page 36)
» Small funnel
» 3 drops geranium rose
  essential oil
» 5 drops grapefruit essential oil
» 5 drops lavender essential oil
» 80ml (5 tablespoons) water
» 30ml (2 tablespoons) vodka

1 Attach the funnel to the
bottle opening.

2 Pour the essential oils
through the funnel into the
bottle, then pour in the vodka.
Fill the rest of the bottle up
with the water.

3 Attach the spray pump and
shake to combine.

Green sources
of inspiration

ONLINE SOURCES

» *One Million Women* Uniting women and girls around the world to fight climate change. An excellent resource for all areas of ethical living including food, energy, money and green cleaning.
1MILLIONWOMEN.COM.AU

» *The Spruce* Full of brilliant recipe ideas, decorating, gardening, crafts and green cleaning tips, The Spruce is a must read.
THESPRUCE.COM

» *Ethical Consumer* An ethical consumer guide that provides detailed research and analysis of the products you purchase. They cover everything from make up and food to fashion as well as household cleaning products.
ETHICALCONSUMER.ORG

» *The Good Shopping Guide*
Helping people to make informed decisions about which brands and companies are best for the planet, animals and communities.
THEGOODSHOPPINGGUIDE.COM

» *Women's Voices for the Earth*
A great resource that raises awareness of the damage toxic chemicals has on our homes, wellbeing and the environment. Includes handy factsheets about the toxins commonly found in cleaning products.
WOMENSVOICES.ORG

» *Going Green* Lisa Bronner's website is packed with information on all aspects of natural living, but her tips for cleaning with castile soap are superb. As the mother of three children, she also shares practical advice for ethical and green family living.
LISABRONNER.COM

DOCUMENTARIES
» *Stink!* Award-winning documentary by Jon Whelan exploring why there are toxins and carcinogens legally hidden in American consumer products.
STINKMOVIE.COM

PODCASTS
» *Low Tox Life* Looking at ways we can reduce toxins in all areas of our life. Alexx Stuart discusses diverse subjects such as GMO food, plastic pollution and saving the planet with experts in their relevant fields. LOWTOXLIFE.COM/PODCAST

» *All Being Well* Kayla Robertson talks to guests on all areas of environmentalism, wellness, vegan food and slow living. ALLBEINGWELL.COM.AU/EPISODES

» *Frugal Friends* A fun podcast hosted by Jen and Jill, two simple living ladies who live frugally. They often discuss sustainable issues, how to use up leftovers and green cleaning recipes. FRUGALFRIENDSPODCAST.COM

» *Live Planted* A great podcast for those starting out on a vegan diet, Alyssa also covers sustainable fashion, zero waste, green cleaning and other environmental issues. LIVEPLANTED.COM/PODCAST

» *Sustainababble* A light-hearted weekly podcast about the environment. Ol and Dave discuss issues such as recycling, hygiene and climate change. They also talk to green entrepreneurs, television personalities and politicians. Always engaging and thought provoking. SUSTAINABABBLE.FISH

INSTAGRAM

» *@simply.living.well* Julia shares her simple living ideas on her beautiful feed. She regularly includes green cleaning recipes, homemade beauty products and recipes.

» *@shedhomewares_e17* A passionate make do and mender who is upcycling her home with salvaged and handmade finds. Carla's feed is full of great ideas to make your home more sustainable.

» *@mayskiesstudio* Catherine is an interior design who believes that a healthy home is good the planet. She shares sustainable design ideas, recycling tips and how to create an eco-home.

SMALL STEPS, BIG CHANGES
less plastic, more organic,
less wanting, more enjoying